# Deal-Making for Good
## By Dick Rathgeber

Dick Rathgeber is the son of a Lutheran minister who takes to heart the idea that people should help the less fortunate. To that end, he routinely gives half his income to non-profits serving the poor, homeless, elderly, medically needy, and abused—to name a few. He also gives land, time, and his considerable influence to enable charities to expand their services. Rathgeber insists that other entrepreneurs can do the same, and in these pages he explains how. Through stories and down-to-earth recollections, Rathgeber lays out the steps he has taken to benefit dozens of groups in the mid-sized city of Austin, Texas. "What I've done here is easily applicable to other cities," he says. "It's not that hard, and I hope others will step up to address the vast needs of America's non-profits. We know that we won't live forever, but we hope that our charitable efforts will."

Rathgeber believes that a philanthropist should take full advantage of the tax laws. To that end, he says, a significant amount of what he has given has been paid for by the IRS.

In 1985, Rathgeber was named the first "Austinite of the Year," and the same year he received the Whitney M. Young Urban League Award. In 1990, he was named Lutheran of the Year in Texas. In 2000, Meals on Wheels awarded him its Keystone Award, while in 2007, Dick and his wife Sara were named "Austin's Best Citizen(s)" in the *Austin Chronicle*'s "Best of Austin" readers' poll. The following year, the Austin Board of Realtors chose the Rathgebers as Austin's Most Worthy Citizens. In addition, Dick received the Daughters of the American Revolution National Community Service Award, and he was named the 2008 Philanthropist of the Year by the National Association of Fundraising Associates for the second time. He has also received numerous other awards.

He's the only civilian to have received all three of the Salvation Army's volunteer awards: the Others Award, the Distinguished Auxiliary Service Award, and the William Booth Award.

---

Janis Williams is a writer and editor whose work has appeared in *The Saturday Evening Post*, *Texas Monthly*, *Texas Highways*, *Poets & Writers*, *Wyoming Wildlife*, and many other publications. *Deal-Making for Good* is her seventh book project. She lives in Austin with her husband, San. They have one son, Edward.

www.janiswilliams.com

# Deal-Making For Good:

## SMART GIVING =
## SIGNIFICANT LIVING

by
# Dick Rathgeber
with Janis Williams

FIRST EDITION
Copyright © 2008
By Dick Rathgeber
Published in the United States of America
By Nortex Press
A Division of Sunbelt Media, Inc.
P.O. Box 21235 ▣ Waco, Texas 76702
e-mail: sales@eakinpress.com
▣ website: www.eakinpress.com ▣
ALL RIGHTS RESERVED.
1  2  3  4  5  6  7  8  9
**ISBN 978-1-934645-68-0**
ISBN 1-934645-68-0
Library of Congress Control Number 2008907875

# Contents

# Foreword

*In a certain city there was a judge who had little respect for either God or man. There was a widow in that same city, and she often came to him, saying, "Please grant me justice against my adversary." And for a while he would not do it: but afterward, he said to himself, This woman is really bothering me, and I know she is not going away. So let her in.*

—Luke 18:1-5 (RSR Version, copyright ©2008)

In philanthropy, the adversary is poverty. Hunger. Homelessness. Sick kids. Individuals and groups who serve these populations are always struggling for money and manpower, and because of this, Dick Rathgeber, a developer and philanthropist in Austin, Texas, identifies with the widow in the passage above.

"She flat wore that judge down," he says with a chuckle. "Who did she think she was? She just kept knocking until he answered her."

As a philanthropist, Rathgeber takes a similar approach. "When I'm asking for money or a favor for a good cause," he says, "the first two 'no's' don't count. They just roll right off me."

Rathgeber is a developer, ideas guy, and major philanthropist in the mid-sized U.S. city that recently landed third from the bottom, in terms of charitable giving, in a ranking of U.S. cities. Yes, according to the *Chronicle of Philanthropy*, and much to the surprise of Austin's citizens, their comfy and beloved hometown has an embarrassingly low rate of charitable giving. However, people in Austin do give of their time. According to a study from the Corporation for National and Community Service, Austin was number three among American cities whose citizens regularly volunteer. And that's important. But Rathgeber thinks nonprofits need both your time and your money.

Dick and his wife, Sara, were recently named "Austin's Most Worthy Citizen(s)" in the *Austin Chronicle's* "Best of Austin" readers' poll. In addition, Dick received the Daughters of the American Revolution National Community Service Award, and he was named Philanthropist of the Year by the National Association of Fundraising Associates this year. He is the only civilian to have received all three of the Salvation Army's volunteer awards: the Others Award, the Distinguished Auxiliary Service Award, and the William Booth Award.

The reason for these plaudits is clear: Rathgeber has applied principles of entrepreneurship honed over fifty years in business to such good causes as the Austin Children's Shelter, Meals on Wheels, People's Community Clinic, and especially the Salvation Army. In fact, the Rathgebers routinely give away half their annual income, in chunks of $50,000 or $500,000 here, $3 million worth of property there.

Even so, Rathgeber, an imposing Texan with the narrow gaze of a man accustomed to giving orders, is not going to waste his time trying to persuade readers to give to charity. If you need persuading, he figures, you'd be better off spending time in self-reflection as to why that is. This irreverent eldest son of a small-town Lutheran minister takes for granted that *everybody will tithe*, at the very least, but he insists, "Tithing's not enough—no matter what your income is."

Easy for him to say. Rathgeber won't admit it, but he's rich. He's one of those shrewd Texans who can smell a deal from a county away, and his nose has led him to piles of money over the years. Here are only a few examples: he and a partner bought and then developed 1,200 residential lots in an upscale West Austin area called Lost Creek. He developed 4,200 residential lots around a golf course in the sprawling Avery Ranch neighborhood northwest of Austin. He is developing Briarcreek, near Manor, an affordable-housing neighborhood that will eventually include more than a thousand single-family dwellings. Meanwhile, he owns part of a building demolition company called Southwest Constructors, which is currently run by his son, Ross Rathgeber.

Yet he protests, "I wouldn't call myself rich. Lots of people have more money than I do."

Wealthy or not, Rathgeber has figured out how to give to charity with the big guys, and he believes others can do the same. "The trick is to take whatever your talents are and use them for charity," he says. "In my case, I guess that's chasing a deal."

Now seventy-five, Rathgeber has been chasing deals in Austin since he was an undergraduate at the University of Texas. "I worked all the way through college," he says, "and graduated with a positive bank balance of $15,000. I didn't owe the university or anybody else a penny." He points out that $15,000 in 1954 was roughly equivalent to $100,000 today.

Not that things have always been smooth for him. In

the 1980s Austin experienced an economic crash, and Rathgeber, along with many of his colleagues in real estate and development, lost everything. Yet even belly-up, he continued to contribute fifty percent of his income to dozens of local and statewide causes. The point, Rathgeber repeats, is that charitable giving shouldn't depend on income.

"'Philanthropy' is a big word in terms of what it suggests to most people," he says in his booming drawl. "People assume all philanthropists have vast fortunes, but that isn't necessarily true. I've noticed that a person who isn't generous with a little isn't generous with a lot."

Rathgeber is practical, though. He knows that a single mother making $35,000 a year will be doing great if she can give *any* money away. "But there's always volunteerism," he says. "When a person volunteers for a charity, that person is saving the organization from having to pay an additional worker. There are dozens of ways to help charities. It's never enough to write a check and walk away."

Rathgeber believes that if you don't have to be rich to be a philanthropist, neither do you have to be especially compassionate, at least in the beginning. "When you give to a cause," he says, "obviously you become invested. You learn more about it. You want to see what your money is doing. You see the needs with your own eyes, and then you want to help." Compassion can *follow* giving, in other words, as well as inspire it.

Over the years, at the same time he has done business on a handshake, Rathgeber has distinguished himself as a curious sort of businessman.

Toby Futrell, Austin city manager from 2002 to 2007, had regular dealings with Rathgeber, and she says, "Dick is a money guy who always makes you ante up for the community. Every time. Every time. He doesn't believe that the bottom line doesn't allow this, so his way of doing business is completely atypical. Every other businessman who steps into this office asks me for the city's help. Dick, though, does just the opposite. He doesn't let a builder come into one of his subdivisions unless that builder contributes to charity. In Dick's scheme, everybody antes up. In his business model, community service is built into the bottom line."

And he's not shy about it. "I view myself as a D8 Dozer without a reverse gear," he says, "and you have three choices when dealing with me. You can get on and ride, you can jump out of the way, or you can get run over. However, when it comes to charity, I view myself as a big wrecker cruising down the highway. I usually don't get called until an organization is in the ditch."

The reason Rathgeber steps up is that he believes the whole structure of nonprofit organizations serving the poor and homeless and children—that entire structure—depends on citizen volunteerism and monetary support.

"If you're not inclined to help," he says, "you have my permission to close this book and turn to the latest how-to-get-rich manual. The people I'm trying to reach want to give, and they want to give to the extent that they make a difference in the world. But even though they have the desire, they might be young and need guidance in getting started. Or they might be older, facing the end of their lives, and trying to figure out what to do with the wealth they have accumulated. As my friend Bob Buford said in his book, *Halftime*, 'You spend the first half of your life trying to be successful, and the second half trying to be significant.'

"The problem is, nobody knows where that halfway

mark is, so now's the time to start supporting charities. Heck, I think we should be teaching young children these principles."

In the following pages, Rathgeber takes it as a given that readers want to share with others—with their church, their favorite nonprofit, the public library, Meals on Wheels—and he gives pointers on large and small steps to significance through giving.

"Lots of people want to contribute," he says. "In this book, I'd like to tell you how I have done it over the years."

—JANIS WILLIAMS

# Job One for the Philanthropist: Build a Business Identity in the Community

Dick Rathgeber believes it's less important how you make your "starter money" than how you make it grow. The key is to expand your sights so that you can spot a genuine need in the community, and then devise a way to fill that need. He illustrates this principle with a story about a man named Alex Spanos.

"This is a guy who started out owning roach coaches, which were vans that went into the fields with sandwiches, drinks, and snacks to feed the migrant workers. They were called roach coaches because sometimes the cleanliness wasn't all it should be. But after Spanos made some money with this work, he began building apartments and selling them, building and selling. Before he knew it, he was a successful apartment mogul and nobody remembered or cared about the roach coaches."

Asked about his own "starter money," Rathgeber says he initially had a wrecking business, a line of work that came about after he met a local wrecking company owner named Q. S. Franks, better known as Peewee.

"This was right after I got back to Austin from the army," Rathgeber says. "Peewee was one of the most fascinating individuals I've ever known. He couldn't read or write, but, boy, was he smart. I figured that anybody who could make a success in a business when he couldn't read or write was in the business I wanted to be in."

Rathgeber's first wrecking job was to tear down St. Martin's Lutheran Church at 13th and Congress, where the Texas Employment Commission Building now stands. "I initially went into business with Peewee's brother, but I soon realized that he had a drinking problem and it was difficult for him to run the job from a beer joint. So I bought him out and continued the business solo, renting the necessary equipment by the hour.

"It wasn't long before I realized that while some of the buildings we were hired to wreck needed to be demolished, others could be moved and renovated. So I began to move some of these houses to lots in East Austin. I would renovate them and sell them, and they made lovely homes for families."

As he was starting out in business, Dick also realized he needed to distinguish himself from others in the city who did similar work. How to accomplish this? He came up with an idea that stuck, which was to run multiple ads in the newspaper, all signed by someone called "High-Dollar Dick." These ads, each of which featured a very bad poem written by Dick, informed the public that if they were looking for someone to move their house, he was their man.

## MR. DICK FOR PRESIDENT

High dollar Dick is number one.
For houses to move he's the favorite son
If you really want to chase poverty
High dollar Dick is the man to see.

### DICK RATHGEHER
GR 2-9991

**Samples**

**of**

# HIGH-DOLLAR DICK

**Ads**

## LUCKY DUTCHMAN

High Dollar Dick is a lucky Joe.
Married the girl he wanted 4 years ago.
If you have a house to move and could use a buck.
Call High Dollar Dick and he can change your luck.

### DICK RATHGEBER
GR 2-9991

## BLOCK-BUSTER

High Dollar Dick buys houses by the block.
For good ones to move, he empties the sock.
If you have a house that needs a move.
The reason for his name — he can quickly prove.

### Dick Rathgeber
GR 2-9991

## BIG SPENDER FROM TEXAS

High Dollar Dick is a great big spender.
For houses to move he will really render.
If you don't know for sure but you've heard this told.
Call High Dollar Dick and you too will be sold.

### DICK RATHGEBER
GR 2-9991

## CRAZY MAN

High dollar Dick has lost his senses,
Buys houses to move like picket fences.
If you have a house that's in the way,
Call High dollar Dick. He'll really pay.

### DICK RATHGEBER
GR 2-9991

Working on the basic principle that, as he says, "you've got to have money before you can give it away," Rathgeber set about establishing himself as a player in the Austin business community. In the process, he learned some useful skills.

"I had bought houses all over the city that needed too much work to sell outright," he explains about his early years in business. "So I bought lots in East Austin and put the houses on them, fixed them up, sold them, and carried the notes myself.

"Before long, I realized I was running out of lots, and around the same time I stumbled across an old platted subdivision that had never been completed. The city had a rule in effect that if I would install the water and sewer, they would pave the streets. So I bought the lots for $300 apiece and persuaded the sellers to pay the cost of the water and sewer in return for interest and a ten percent bonus. I bought thirty-one lots at one time under that arrangement, and I remember saying to myself, All my life I've heard about people trying to expand too fast, and I wonder if that is what I'm doing. It made me nervous to do so much so quickly. Besides, I soon realized that fixing up houses and having to deal with subcontractors was very time-consuming.

"I also became aware that there was a strong market for finished lots. A man named Vic Schmidt was head of Water and Wastewater for the City of Austin at that time, and I got him to sell me a copy of the city's drainage plan outlining where all the sewer treatment plants were and the areas that were drained by these plants. My research also revealed that there was a program in effect whereby the federal government would reimburse the city eighty-two percent of the cost of extending the wastewater line, in return for the city's paying the remaining eighteen percent. I gave the matter some thought and decided to make a deal with the city to pay the eighteen percent, just to expedite matters. When the paper subsequently printed the story that the city was extending sewer lines to a certain area, my phone started ringing. A lot of these properties would have been nice to hold on to, especially two-thirds of the right-of-way of William Cannon Drive between I-35 and Manchaca Road. But I stuck with my plan: as soon as each property doubled in value, I sold it and moved on to something else.

"In this way, I learned the subdividing business."

DICK HAD A THRIVING BUSINESS, but he continued to keep his eye open for new opportunities. "I've always loved to chase a deal," he says, "and I continued buying property all around the city. Soon after I bought a piece of land on South First Street, I determined that this area was a little different. I decided the neighborhood was too good to move houses to. I was approached by Don West, a local builder, who suggested we develop the land jointly as a subdivision.

"Anytime you start developing a subdivision, you're going to meet up with the neighborhood characters. Well, we needed a sewer easement across some land owned by Rev. A. D. Eberhart, a Baptist preacher whose church was called Pleasant Hill Baptist Church. Rev. Eberhart was known locally as the 'burying preacher.' He worked with the local funeral homes, and if a family did not have a religious affiliation, he performed the service for them. I knew him because he had officiated at the funeral service for one of my workmen a year or so earlier. The deceased was a fellow who'd lived a very checkered life and who had been killed in a dump truck wreck early one Saturday morning as he made his way home from the beer joint. As I drove to that funeral, I wondered what in the world the minister was going to find to say about the man. Rev. Eberhart used the text, 'A bruised reed shall he not break, and the smoking flax shall he not quench.' The reverend did a beautiful job, saying that, although old Alvin had not led an exactly exemplary life, it could be hoped that he had enough faith to get him home.

"Now flash forward to the time I needed the sewer easement on Rev. Eberhart's personal property. When I met him, I mentioned that occasion when I'd first heard him preach. During our conversation, I quoted his text back to him. He was utterly amazed, and he said the sewer easement would be no problem. After that we became good friends. He was an avid hunter, and Ross, another friend, and I even took him to Africa to hunt birds."

Dick's ability to meet people on their own terms served him well in developing this subdivision, today known as Buckingham Place, which is located at South First and William Cannon Drive. And Dick's people skills continue to be one of his chief assets in business.

Another is his restless energy. Rathgeber's pattern has been that as soon as he finishes one complicated, multifaceted project, he's on to the next big deal.

He strongly believes that good business can be conducted even if the entrepreneur doesn't have a lot of cash reserves. He illustrates this by recollecting the fellow he knew as Papa Ted. "Papa Ted Wendlandt was a longtime Austin real estate man who had no children, so he treated me like a son. Our first encounter was early in my career, when I bought some property from him. We made the deal on a handshake. Papa Ted belonged to a group called Austin Enterprises, which was made up of ten very prominent Austin citizens who invested in projects so that they would have enough money to take their wives on good trips. With Papa Ted's backing, I was able to take on nearly any size project, no matter what the cash requirements were. Our deal was, I paid the Austin Enterprise Group ten percent interest on their money, plus half the profits once everything was paid off. Using this arrangement, we bought various properties around the city. One such was a 600-acre parcel on Onion Creek and William Cannon. We paid cash for that."

Around this time, Rathgeber says, he perfected the principle of OPM, or "Other People's Money." He explains, "I always used my OPM formula with Nelson Puett, Roy Butler, and John Byram. I like to illustrate the basic principle by calling to mind a long, thin watermelon. First you cut the interest off one end, then you cut all the principal off the other end. Once that's done, you roll the melon over and split it down the middle. This is fair to both parties."

One early business experience underlined the efficacy of OPM for Rathgeber. "My first time to serve on a bank board was with Citizens National Bank," he says. "A fellow church member, Monroe Bethke, was president of that bank, and Joe Long was chairman of the board. Citizens had repossessed a 25-unit condo project at Lago Vista, on Lake Travis, but they hadn't been able to sell a single unit. Part of the problem was that the condos had shoddy construction on the exterior, using material that was so flimsy you could kick in a hole with your boot. A second problem was their appearance. The condos had single-slope roofs, what I called 'chicken coop roofs.' To say they were ugly is to be kind about it.

"Anyway, Citizens Bank had repossessed these condos, and at one of the board meetings, we were discussing what in the world to do with them. In fact, our discussion centered on how much it would cost to remove a dead horse, because an old horse had actually wandered into one of the condos and died. That should tell you how useless that property was to the bank.

"Well, after the meeting, I asked to talk to Monroe and Joe in private. I said if somebody came in and offered them $250,000 cash for the whole project, they ought to hug the buyer's neck. Then I said I would buy the condos myself, on condition that the bank would put the project into a joint venture, interest free, and then make a loan up to $300,000 so I could rehab the place. The bank would, of course, earn interest on the rehab part of the loan.

"I jumped right into renovating the condominiums. Around this time, a company called National Resorts Community was selling lots in the same area to planeloads of people who were flown down from the North. Prospective buyers usually came in on the weekend, which meant that during the week, the salesmen had nothing to do. So they would hang around my condo project and offer me advice, saying, 'It'll take you about three years to sell all these units.'

"However, as soon as I had those condos in respectable condition, I started running a block ad in the sports section of the Friday edition of the *Houston Post*. The ad read: 'Bank liquidation of condos. Buy one for a fraction of the cost. Call Mr. Dick the Liquidator.'

"We sold all twenty-five units in thirty days, and we had three backup contracts. 'Early to bed, early to rise. Work like hell, and advertise.' That's what I always say."

SOON AFTER THE LAGO VISTA PROJECT WAS FINISHED, Dick moved on to develop the Lost Creek subdivision. That experience provides another example of his way of doing business. "I had become friends with a professional golfer named Terry Dill," he says, "and in a conversation one day in the mid-1970s, Terry told me that it was his lifelong ambition to develop his own golf course. He had found a large piece of land on Barton Creek, south and west of Westlake Hills. The property seemed really remote at the time, because Loop 360 had not yet been constructed, and the only access to the property was by way of a very rocky road coming from the back side through Oak Hill. Terry and I decided to become partners and develop the subdivision, which wouldn't have been possible if not for the fact that Loop 360 was planned and construction was about to begin. So Terry and I went forward. He let his wife name the subdivision, and she called it Lost Creek.

"As always, there were details to be worked out. We created the first municipal utility district in Travis County and put in a sewer treatment plant, with the effluent being used to water the golf course."

Rathgeber and Dill were well along in their plans for developing Lost Creek, and things were going smoothly. Then history intervened—and things got even better.

"The Austin Independent School District instituted busing to comply with a court order. West Lake High School had been built by this time, and people were eager to live in Lost Creek so that their children could go to school in the Eanes Independent School District. By the time we got to the third division of the subdivision, prices for our lots had shot up from $16,000 or $17,000 to $45,000 to $50,000. The demand was so much greater than our supply that we decided to hold a raffle based on the NFL draft system. We tried to limit our sales to builders, but I know we had a few individuals slip in. Here's how we did it. We fed potential buyers a prime rib lunch at the new Lost Creek Country Club. After everyone finished eating, we instructed them to reach their hands into a hat and draw out a poker chip with a number on it. All the lots had been priced previously, and there were stories of draft rights being traded for between $1,000 and $2,000 apiece just to move up in line. It was crazy. We sold $4.5 million worth of lots in forty-two minutes that day. We told buyers they had seventy-two hours to pay ten percent down. Bankers wanted to know if I needed a development loan and I said no, because the down payments and the cash payments for lots would pay the development costs.

"That was my first really big lick."

# Build a Philanthropic Identity in Your Community

If there's one thing that Rathgeber likes as much as chasing a deal, it's finding a solution for seemingly insoluble problems. "I just like to solve problems," he admits, "but it seems like those with easy answers have already been taken care of. I tend to wind up with the tough ones."

In the early 1980s, one such problem had downtown businesspeople, city officials, and the leaders of the Salvation Army all scratching their heads. The question concerned where to place the Salvation Army shelter for the homeless. Of course the shelter needed to be centrally located so that the people who needed it most could find it. But there were challenges.

"Finding a place for the Salvation Army was so controversial that the mayor and the city council appointed a task force of twelve people to figure it out," Dick recalls. "I was appointed to that task force without even knowing it. I found out about it when I read my name in the paper. At the time I was chairman of the Salvation Army's advisory board. Anyway, this task force was made up of representatives from all parts of the community, including the Sixth Street bar owners group.

"For a while there, it looked as though there was no solution. There were not many appropriate pieces of land downtown, and furthermore, nobody wanted the homeless as a neighbor to their business."

Eventually the task force chose a downtown location—the corner of 8th and Neches—that was in close proximity to the police station.

Rathgeber says, "It's always good to have the police near a homeless shelter, so for many reasons this property seemed right. But there was a problem. The site was owned by a long-established Austin family, the Josephs, and they wanted $3 million for it. The Salvation Army had only $1 million cash to spend.

"I'd never met Johnny Joseph, but I knew of him. He was from an old Lebanese family that lived downtown. The family started out with a grocery store and wound up owning a bar on Red River, with card games upstairs. Everybody knew you could go there and gamble if you wanted to.

"So I called Johnny up and asked him if he'd go for a ride with me. I told him I wanted to show him some land. We took off in my Thunderbird, driving out to the 620 and Mansfield Dam area. 'Uncle Johnny,' I told him, 'the Salvation Army has a problem. There are only two people in Austin who can solve it, and they're both in this car.'

"I told him what we needed, and then I showed him a map. I said, 'Draw a line on here that indicates how much of this land you want, plus $1 million cash, in exchange for that downtown site.' He pointed out what he wanted and it seemed reasonable to me, so I immediately started drawing out a real estate contract right there on the plat. I wrote, *'I, John Joseph, hereby agree to accept $1,000,000 cash and approximately 100 acres of land in exchange for my downtown site at 8th & Neches.'* But I was so excited that I wrote out a thousand dollars instead of a million. Johnny tapped me on the shoulder and said, 'Papa, you're three zeros short.' I changed that, we shook hands, and we had a deal."

Soon after, a newspaper reporter named Steve Reed phoned Rathgeber. He had gotten wind of Dick's deal with the Joseph family, and he wanted confirmation. "The Salvation Army happened to be Steve's beat," Dick recalls, "and this is when I determined that newspaper people have a real code of ethics. Steve called me, and he asked what was happening with the Salvation Army site. I replied that we were off the record. I said, 'You can't print any of this until after the city council meeting next week.' Then I told him what I was proposing, contingent upon the city council's issuing us a building permit for the Salvation Army to build a shelter for the homeless.

"So Steve did all the fact checking, wrote his story, and then waited." However, the controversy wasn't over yet.

"What happened next was that issues of separation of church and state emerged. At that time, the infamous atheist Madelyn Murray O'Hair was prominent in Austin, and she was ready to pounce if the city provided funds, because the Salvation Army is a church. At the meeting, Councilman Mark Rose asked, when he heard the terms of the deal I'd struck, 'Does this mean that the City of Austin doesn't have to pay the $2 million difference in price?'

"I said, 'Mr. Rose, you are correct. The city will owe nothing under this deal.' At that point, O'Hair had no grounds for complaint."

When Steve Reed's story came out in the *Austin*

*American-Statesman*, it was front page news. "To the average reader, it looked as though I had made a $2 million donation," Dick says. "In fact, though, I had just contributed some land that was in a partnership, and actually, to me it was the worst part of the land. But it happened to be in a fine location."

That deal put the Rathgebers on the map in terms of philanthropy. "After that, people started coming to me to solve their problems, so I never lacked for charitable projects."

As is always the case in matters of social service, need eventually outweighs provision, and within a few years the downtown Salvation Army facility was bursting at the seams. "The facility was great, but it just wasn't able to serve everybody who needed it," Rathgeber says. "By that time, Kirk Watson was the popular mayor of Austin, and he identified the need to open a city-run homeless shelter to supplement the services offered by the Salvation Army."

Downtown land acquisitions are dicey in any city, but Austin in the mid-1980s was booming and sites were at a premium. Add to that the old news that businesses were wary of having the homeless as a neighbor, and Mayor Watson had a problem on his hands. To address the situation, the mayor appointed a blue-ribbon committee, headed by former mayor Frank Cooksey, to find a space for a new city-owned homeless shelter.

Since Dick had had experience with finding a spot for the earlier facility, he knew what lay ahead for Cooksey and his committee. "I watched with great amusement, having been through the debacle of trying to find that original location," he says. "I believed the only place the new shelter could possibly go would be right next to the existing one. I was aware that the Salvation Army owned the quarter-block adjacent to their facility. They liked owning the land, but they weren't using it. They'd only bought it because it came up for sale, and they thought they might need it for future expansion. Well, the future was now, and I kept thinking that if the city was willing to buy the property and build an additional facility right there, everyone would benefit. However, I wasn't on the mayor's committee, and for all I knew they had some other plan in mind. So I kept quiet and stayed up to date with the scuttlebutt through word on the street and articles in the newspaper.

"As the months passed and no good site showed up, I read that the mayor was becoming frustrated. One day I happened to be in a meeting where he was, and I thought, No time like the present to run my idea past him. So I motioned for him to come down from the dais. 'I have something to tell you,' I said. I told him the Salvation Army had some land, and that I thought it was where the new facility needed to go.

"After that, Mayor Watson and I met with various homeless groups and the Salvation Army, and we negotiated for twenty-two months on the basis that the city would build the facility and the Salvation Army would operate it. The problem was, Salvation Army officials were adamantly opposed to selling the property. By contrast, the local advisory board, which is made up of non-member civic leaders, realized that the proposed additional shelter probably constituted the highest and best use for that piece of land. Since Salvation Army officials cannot make major decisions without the approval of the local advisory board, we were in a standoff.

"Finally, after nearly two years of wheel-spinning, one of the assistant city managers suggested the possibility of condemning the property. I thought about this for a fraction of a second, and I said, 'That's a good idea. Just go ahead.'

"You see, if the land was condemned, the Salvation Army would be forced to sell it to the city for the additional shelter."

The city did move to condemn the property, and afterward, Dick set about being sure that the Salvation Army got a fair price. "When the issue came up on the city council agenda," he says, "I took a copy of the agenda to the newspaper and asked to see Arnold Garcia, one of the editors. I asked him to bring his best reporter to the meeting. Pete Palazzari, the local Salvation Army advisory board chairman, went with me. Arnold's best reporter turned out to be Leah Quinn. We told these journalists that we didn't want a story to be written about the condemnation of that property, because we thought the public would misunderstand. 'It's not the city's fault,' we told the reporters. 'They negotiated in good faith.'

"So the City of Austin got the first appraisal. I nosed around and found out who the appraiser was, and I told him, 'We don't want any lowball numbers on this,' so he came in with a very fair price. Then we got another appraisal for the benefit of the Salvation Army, and it was a quarter of a million dollars lower than the city had offered. The Salvation Army had paid $320,000 for the property and now, three years later, they were getting $1,360,000."

One funny story serves as an epilogue to this. Dick says, "The local Salvation Army officer retired in Oklahoma City a few years later, and he asked me to speak at his retirement ceremony. I gave him credit for buying a piece of land for $320,000 and selling it only three years later for more than four times that. I told the audience that I was trying to get the officer to teach me how to invest in real estate and get that kind of return. He did not disclaim credit, but he did say, 'Whatever I was able to accomplish, I had this man'—and he pointed to me–'right behind me.'"

Another result of the sale's going through without court intervention is that a natural alliance grew up between the city and the Salvation Army. Both, after all, had the same goal in mind. This partnership led to other mutually rewarding projects. For example, the City of Austin gave the Salvation Army use of a $2 million former Battered Women Center building in deep East Austin. The city then paid another $1 million to renovate it, and the city is giving the Salvation Army an annual $1.4 million to operate it. This means that seventy-five women and children have been moved out of the downtown homeless shelter, where they had been sharing space with homeless men.

How had such a mutually beneficial deal, between two entities that had formerly butted heads, come about? "Well, it turns out that Mayor Watson's son and my grandson were great buddies," Rathgeber says, "so he and I saw each other at the occasional baseball game or whatever. We had a relationship outside the business world. Naturally, our conversation about the downtown homeless people continued. We both understood that if the Salvation Army 'made nice' about the land acquisition, the city might look kindly on another idea that had occurred to me, which was this: The women's shelter was inadequate and wanted to move. I thought, Why not use that building for the women and children from the downtown homeless shelter? Get them out of downtown and to a safer environment. In an amazing coincidence, that's exactly what happened.

"Over time, this deal could easily amount to more than $50 million in benefits to the Salvation Army, and yet bureaucrats in Atlanta tried to turn it down at least three times, because they believed it was against Salvation Army policy to operate programs in leased space."

After the first turn-down, Rathgeber called the retired national commander of the Salvation Army, who was a good friend. "I asked him what options I had to keep this deal from going in the ditch. He said the board at territorial headquarters in Atlanta was required to grant me a hearing with their entire board.

"What was happening was that Austin officials were sending documents to Atlanta to be signed to seal the deal. Then the city would get a letter back saying that the Salvation Army wasn't going to sign. So I would call Atlanta and request to be added to the agenda of the next meeting. This happened three times, with three different documents, and each time Atlanta would call me back the next day and say that it wasn't necessary for me to come, because they had changed their minds."

# Partner with the Press

Rathgeber knows that successful community projects require wide public support, and that such support comes from a positive public attitude toward the project. The success of large philanthropic efforts, such as the ones described in these pages, depends on that kind of support from the public.

"It all comes down to the media," says Rathgeber. "If an effort affecting the larger community is going to progress smoothly, it will be because there's popular support for it. To get that support, you have to have the media behind you."

By "media," Rathgeber principally means the local newspaper—in his case, the *Austin American-Statesman*. On more than one occasion, Rathgeber has selected a reporter ahead of time and given him or her all the details on a breaking story of widespread interest—just the kind of story every reporter hopes to get. But he provides this information on the condition that the reporter will not release the story until the deal is final.

"It goes without saying that the media is going to cover a story like the Salvation Army land deal or the moving of the children's hospital to the Mueller development," he says. "It's going to be in the paper, obviously. If you want the straight story out there, you have to cooperate with the media. I see this as a mutually advantageous process. By getting the facts ahead of time, a reporter can get the story written, fact-checked, polished, and ready to print as soon as the deal is sealed. The philanthropist, meantime, can be assured that the facts are straight and the dots connected for the public.

"I've never understood people who say, 'Oh, I don't talk to the press.' The way I look at it, reporters are *going* to get the story, one way or the other. That's their job. If you don't talk to them, they can just as easily talk to your worst enemy."

When the Salvation Army and Johnny Joseph came to terms on the location, the *Statesman* story came out, just as planned. This approach has always worked for Rathgeber, who takes what he calls a "John the Baptist" approach to getting the facts out. By that he means that he prepares the way. In a story such as the one on relocating the children's hospital, for example, Rathgeber told representatives of the hospital, the Mueller redevelopment project, and the city to expect a call from reporter Mary Ann Roser, and he asked for permission to pass their cell phone numbers along to Roser. "I want to make it easy for reporters to talk to all the players," he explains. "That way, the full and accurate story is more likely to find its way into print."

Rathgeber has worked with writers on all kinds of beats—religion, business, health care, metro—and reporters say they get a kick out of Rathgeber's colloquialisms, which spice up any story. In one write-up, for example, he described someone who wasn't very knowledgeable by saying, "That fellow's more foam than beer."

Recently he has worked most often with a reporter at the *American-Statesman*, Shonda Novak, whose beat is real estate. "I've found Dick to be an invaluable resource," Novak says. "He's completely accessible (and continues to work tirelessly to teach me to return calls within his fifteen-minute rule), and he's always willing to take the time to explain complex matters to me. Not having covered real estate before, I faced a steep learning curve when I got here in late 2000. Since that time, he has helped me learn not only who's who in the business, but the intricacies of real estate as well. He's also willing to give me quotes on stories that have no bearing on his current projects, but that require the insights and perspective of a seasoned real estate veteran."

Rathgeber says, "Shonda has flair as a writer, and she's a stickler for detail. She keeps working until she gets all the facts straight."

Rathgeber is aware of journalistic ethics, and he respects them. "A journalist's job is to be objective and fair," he says. "People tend to be skeptical of the press, but the truth is, we're on the same side. Reporters and I, for example, want the same thing, which is to inform the public about worthy projects and, when possible, get other people involved. Ideally, a public person should try to create a partnership with the press, a partnership in which both parties give and both parties receive. Reporters need good quotes to liven up and verify their stories. People like me need to publicize philanthropic deals in order to generate popular support. If I help a reporter get his or her facts right, he or she will write a better story, and it will be one the public can depend on as factual. Ultimately, the public is the beneficiary."

Rathgeber contends that there are straightforward rules for dealing with the press, and he says, "You just have to set your terms at the outset. When you are first talking to a reporter, tell him or her that you're off the record. The reporter will honor that. Where people get in trouble is when they come back after a story has been written and try to disavow what they said on the record.

"Reporters live on tips, and they are savvy about the difference between a genuine tip and a promotion. Some people go out and hire public relations firms to promote their latest enterprise. A good reporter can smell that from a mile away. Nobody needs to read another puff piece. My advice is to establish the ground rules before you start talking. A good reporter will honor your request to be off the record, and he or she will also agree to withhold a public story until it's official. That's how the game is played."

Rathgeber goes one step further. "After a story runs, it's nice to call the reporter up and congratulate him or her. Better yet, call the reporter's editor, and tell that person what a good job the writer did. Follow up. It's just good manners."

BEYOND GETTING THE DETAILS of his favorite project out into the public, Rathgeber has noticed other benefits of forging a good relationship with the press. He says, "Three years ago, a reporter I knew, Michelle Breyer, was about to retire. I had been approached several times about having a profile written on me. I definitely wanted Michelle to do it if anyone did, because I'd worked with her before, and I had full confidence in her journalistic abilities." What follows is the result of that interview.

---

*'To be significant, you have to give'*

## Philanthropist works artful deals to the benefit of those in need

by R. Michelle Breyer
*Austin American-Statesman*

Sunday, December 19, 2004

Over the years, developer Terry Mitchell has become accustomed to getting long-distance calls from his friend Dick Rathgeber.

They go something like this:

"Dick, where are you?" Mitchell asks.

"I'm on my way to Honduras," Rathgeber says. "I heard Hurricane Mitch left hundreds of people without homes. We're gonna build them some."

"Why are you doing that?" Mitchell asks.

"Well, Terry, they need them," he answers.

Or: "I'm in Wichita Falls raising money for a hospitality house," Rathgeber says.

"Why are you doing that, Dick?"

"Because they need it."

For three decades, the plainspoken, gregarious bulldog of a man has worked passionately to help people in need, including a long list of Central Texas organizations such as Meals on Wheels, the Girl Scouts and the Salvation Army.

(Continued on next page)

He applies his formidable energy, his deal-making prowess, his powerful connections and his money to solve problems, including those that seem unsolvable, working usually behind the scenes and often without being asked.

"When he has his eye on something, he gets it done," said Greg Weaver, a vice president of Catellus Development Corp., which is overseeing the redevelopment of Austin's former Robert Mueller Municipal Airport. "You say, 'Watch out; here comes Dick.'"

Rathgeber is as extroverted as they come, with chutzpah to spare. He isn't afraid to call in chits, twist arms or ruffle feathers. And he's not shy about butting in if he sees a problem he can fix.

"I'm not a jolly do-gooder," the veteran developer insists in his West Texas drawl. "I'm a deal junkie. If you see a deal that's in the ditch and you can fix it with a little money or expertise, that's what you should be doing."

Last week, Rathgeber finalized his latest contribution, 16 acres adjacent to Mueller for a campus for as many as six organizations serving children, including a new Austin Children's Shelter and an expanded Scottish Rite Learning Center for children with dyslexia.

"It's expensive property," said former Texas Supreme Court Justice Jack Hightower, chairman of the learning center. "For that to be donated is a tremendous help. Mr. Rathgeber is just an angel."

Rathgeber invested more than $200,000 of his own money to put in water and sewer systems for a flood-ravaged Honduran town, donating an ambulance and fire truck as well. He was the catalyst behind the Williamson County Regional Trail, a wilderness trail that will run from Cedar Park to Dell Diamond in Round Rock. (Continued on next page)

A pool is being built at the East Metro Park near Manor, thanks to a $125,000 donation from Rathgeber, which enabled the park to obtain nearly $1 million in additional funding.

His work on the expansion of People's Community Clinic became the subject of a case study on philanthropy at Harvard's Kennedy School of Government.

"Dick's gifts are his ability to see the objective clearly and then to have an understanding of the practical dynamics of getting from point A to point B," said Charles Barnett, chief executive officer of the Seton Healthcare Network. "He is tireless in that."

And his work is infectious.

"If you hang around Dick, you're going to learn to give," said Jim Boles, owner of Summit Commercial Industrial Property, who has done real estate deals with Rathgeber. "He's totally unashamed about asking."

It's easy to give time and money to popular causes, but Rathgeber is unafraid to take on controversial ones.

When pressure from anti-abortion activists caused contractors to walk off the job at Planned Parenthood's South Austin health clinic in November 2003, the project came to a halt. Rathgeber got the call to help.

A deeply religious man, he agonized over the decision and had a long talk with his pastor at St. Martin's Lutheran Church.

Rathgeber decided it was the right thing to do and helped the organization get money back from the original contractor as well as find a contractor willing to finish the job.

"I strongly believe in the rights of poor people to health care, including birth control," Rathgeber said. "I had to do something."

(Continued on next page)

## Setting an Example

Across the country, charitable giving has suffered, and many agencies have had to slash budgets.

"I've worked in nonprofits for 25 years, and the last four have been the most difficult in my career," said David Balch, president of the United Way Capital Area.

In Austin, which ranked seventh in the *Chronicle of Philanthropy*'s list of the 10 stingiest cities based on household charitable donations in 1997, the challenge has been especially daunting. Last year, Balch said, the United Way had to cut funding to agencies by 20 percent.

"We have a lot of abundance out there," Balch said. "We just haven't figured out how to tap into it."

That's why Rathgeber's deeds are especially important, Balch said.

"Dick, through his time and his resources, sets an incredible example for the community."

Rathgeber said his life is based on a simple premise: "It's really not your money. You're just managing it for a little while. So you better invest it wisely. If it was really yours, you could take it with you."

He estimates his donations over the past 20 years at "north of $10 million," including land.

Rathgeber's connections and willingness to get into the trenches might be even more important than the money. His mental Rolodex includes the phone numbers of dozens of the city's most powerful people.

"He knows everybody," said Julia Spann, director of Caritas. "He knows policy-makers; he knows decision-makers; he knows the social services organizations; he knows everybody in the construction industry. He does a lot himself, and he asks them to do the same."

(Continued on next page)

Rathgeber sees it differently: "I'm giving them the opportunity for significance."

Rathgeber likes to quote Bob Buford, a Christian author, who says that most people spend the first half of their life being successful and the last half being significant.

"To be significant, you have to give, either your time or money," Rathgeber said. "If you can combine time and money, you've got a double shot at it."

### 'Good for everybody'

He wasn't always that way. In fact, he spent much of his life thinking charity was something you did at church.

Then, 25 years ago, he saw Austin builder John McPhaul on *60 Minutes* talking about what he had done for the Center for Battered Women, now SafePlace.

The center had been leasing a house from the city for $1 a year, but it needed significant work. McPhaul didn't have a lot of money, but he had connections and construction experience.

He recruited the local homebuilding association to build a bigger facility in East Austin, the first battered women's shelter ever built in the United States.

"Well, I can do something like that," Rathgeber said to himself.

His first project was the League House, a concept pioneered in Austin by former Seton Hospital CEO Sister Mary Rose McPhee, with Rathgeber's help.

McPhee wanted to provide affordable accommodations for families of critically ill patients.

To get the project started, Rathgeber donated a vacant apartment building. Seton later renovated an old medical

(Continued on next page)

warehouse. Eventually, a new house was built nearby just south of Seton Hospital.

"She had the idea," he said of McPhee. "I showed her how to do it."

The Salvation Army was his next project.

In the early 1980s, the organization was having trouble finding a place for a downtown shelter. Land on Eighth Street was attractive but too expensive.

Rathgeber, who was chairman of the board, owned land near the Oasis restaurant on Lake Travis that he knew was valuable. So Rathgeber got together with John Joseph, whose family owned the Eighth Street site.

"I told him, 'The Salvation Army has a problem, and only two people can solve it, and they're both in this car,'" he recalled.

They arranged a swap, drawing up the contract on the spot: Joseph would get $1 million in cash and 100 acres from Rathgeber, and the Salvation Army would get the $3 million downtown land.

"Everybody wound up happy," Rathgeber said. "My basic premise of business is, a deal has to be good for everybody or it won't be a good deal for anybody."

He calls his shining moment his work in getting a new children's hospital at Mueller.

Seton had purchased land for a new hospital at Interstate 35 and Parmer Lane, believing that the Mueller project, its first choice, would never be ready in time for a much-needed expansion.

But the new hospital would be hard for many patients to reach, and doctors weren't happy about a location so far from the existing facility.

(Continued on next page)

Rathgeber strongly believed that the hospital needed to be at Mueller. So he took it upon himself to call a meeting of city officials, Seton executives and Catellus' Weaver.

"They didn't want to come to a meeting," Rathgeber recalled. "I said, 'We're going to have this meeting.'"

Weaver, for one, was skeptical that anything could be done.

"It was such a long shot," he said. But Rathgeber got people to lay out their concerns and find a way around them. An hour later, there was a deal.

Ground was broken this year, and the $200 million hospital is expected to open in 2007.

"He got a lot of people in one room to sit down and talk about something he thought was for the greater good," Weaver said. "He had nothing to gain."

### An understanding

Rathgeber is a multi-tasker extraordinaire who always seems to have several deals going at once, not to mention twice-weekly tennis dates and hours spent at his Vulcan commercial-grade stove in his Tarrytown kitchen, cooking up pots of vegetable beef soup, ribs and baked beans.

As he drives around town in his coral-colored 2003 Ford Thunderbird convertible, he's usually talking to a business associate or a nonprofit organization or checking in on sick and elderly friends and relatives.

He can't stand dead time.

"I can't imagine a man balancing as many balls as he does in the air," McPhaul said. "He ought to be twins or triplets."

Two years ago, the Settlement Home Garage Sale hit

(Continued on next page)

hard times after the event moved from the City Coliseum to Palmer Auditorium, where people had to pay $7 for parking. In 2002, admissions plummeted 60 percent, sales were off by $150,000, and piles of goods were left after the event ended. It is the biggest annual fund raiser for the Settlement Home, which serves troubled girls.

Rathgeber looked at the event as he would any business deal. He determined that the parking fee and admission charge kept many potential customers away.

So he gave the city $7,000 so the parking for the three-day event could be free. He found a sponsor so admission could be free Saturday and Sunday and got homebuilder D.R. Horton to pay to advertise the event.

The group raised $420,000 in 2003, compared with $250,000 the previous year.

"He understands business so well, but very few people in that position are willing to share that knowledge with people who need help," said Betty King, who has worked with Rathgeber on projects for the Settlement Home and the Girl Scouts. "He is a great hero to us."

### A born deal-maker

Rathgeber was born 71 years ago in Corpus Christi, the son of a Lutheran minister and the oldest of six children.

After attending college for two years in Wichita Falls, he headed to the University of Texas.

His penchant for deal-making was apparent early on, whether he was selling hay to ranchers during high school or cookware in college. He graduated from U.T. with no debt and a net worth of $15,000: more than $100,000 in today's dollars.

(Continued on next page)

After stints in the Army and the pesticide business, he got into real estate, selling houses for Nash Phillips/Copus Inc., then one of the largest private builders in the country.

He started his own business, buying, moving and selling homes, and he still has the demolition part of that enterprise, Southwest Constructors.

Then he got into development, with subdivisions including Lost Creek, Avery Ranch and Briarcreek. He's working on a subdivision near Dripping Springs, the Headwaters at Barton Creek, that will include a 1,000-acre wilderness preserve.

"I'm not averse to making money," he stressed. "If you don't make a profit, you don't have anything to give away."

He has known adversity, losing 90 percent of his net worth in 1990 as Austin's real estate market came crashing down.

He and Sara, his wife of 44 years, are opposites in many ways: She's good with details, he's a big-picture guy; she's more reserved while he is an extreme extrovert. But their marriage works.

"She's knocked some edges off me," Rathgeber said.

After all these years, he still amazes and sometimes exasperates her.

"He's always doing something," she said. "Sometimes you just want to say, 'Stop!'

"I wake up every day not knowing what will happen," she said. "It's certainly not boring."

They live well but not extravagantly. Their home is luxurious but not ostentatious. They share a river house in New Braunfels with another couple and travel to places such as India and Egypt.

(Continued on next page)

The Rathgebers have two daughters and a son as well as seven grandchildren. His children all are involved in community organizations. His daughter Gretchen Ellis just took over as chairwoman of the endowment at SafePlace.

"He's passing it down," Sara Rathgeber said.

### In his prime

Rathgeber feels that he's just hitting his stride.

"I'm not about to retire," he said. "I'm having too much fun. And it's taken me too long to get to the point where people return my phone calls."

But he knows there are other people with the ability to do what he does, and he'd like to be a role model.

"I know I've become a better giver," Boles said. "You raise your sights when you watch the master at work. He's kind of contagious."

Terry Mitchell, a developer and former executive of Milburn Homes, said that working with Rathgeber has caused him to look at things in a new way.

Mitchell said he was involved in a long, complex negotiation to buy 2,000 lots from Rathgeber and partner Roy Butler at Avery Ranch in 2001. As the deal neared completion, Rathgeber added a non-negotiable condition: For every house sold, Milburn would have to donate at least $100 to charity, an amount that Rathgeber would match.

"I was shocked," Mitchell recalled. "I'd never heard anything like that. I thought, what a wonderful thing."

So far, the approach has raised nearly $1 million for charity. Mitchell plans to copy the idea at his own new subdivision in South Austin.

John Avery credits Rathgeber with being the inspiration

(Continued on next page)

for his family's decision to donate 101 acres of land in Round Rock for a higher education center that will include facilities for Texas State University and Austin Community College.

"We probably wouldn't have done this had it not been for Dick Rathgeber's philanthropic example," Avery said. "Early on, he told me his reason for being in business was to be in a position to help others. The joy we've gotten from making this donation is hard to describe."

# Locate Your Natural Allies

A major principle of philanthropy is broad cooperation. No project of significance is pulled off by a single person or company, so a nonprofit or charity depends on the combined efforts of like-minded people. A common vehicle for such giving is the church. Churches, temples, mosques, and other places of worship provide opportunities for people to combine resources for a common goal.

"I was almost forty years old before I realized that charity could be viable even if it wasn't Lutheran," says Rathgeber with a laugh. "Before that, almost all my charitable efforts had gone into Lutheran projects. Then sometime in the mid-1970s I became acquainted with Austin attorney Tom Curtis, when he represented me and some partners in a zoning case. During one of our conversations, Tom told me that he had advised his wife, Carolyn, then president of the Austin Junior League, to ask for my help with the Junior League's latest charitable effort."

Carolyn took her husband's advice and called Rathgeber. She asked him to meet with her, several other

Junior League members, and Sister Mary Rose McPhee, then CEO of Seton Hospital. "I agreed to the meeting," says Rathgeber. "I knew Sister Mary Rose through various community causes. As for Carolyn, from the first time I met her, I considered her one of the brightest people in Austin."

Dick says that when they all sat down, Sister Mary Rose explained that she had a concern that she hoped this group could help her address. "She told us that she had been noticing a large number of family members sleeping in waiting rooms at the hospital, especially when a loved one was in intensive care. Sister had the idea of creating a home away from home for these family members, a place where they could stay while their loved ones were being treated. She had approached Carolyn to see whether the Junior League would get involved. When the three of us met, she asked if I had ideas for how to get the ball rolling."

That initial meeting with Sister Mary Rose, Carolyn, and other members of the Junior League took place in the early summer of 1981. "Sister's proposal struck me as an idea whose time had come," recalls Dick.

During that meeting, Austin's first hospitality house became a reality, at least in its most rudimentary form. "We got it started within seventy-two hours of that conversation," says Dick, "because, as it happened, I had some apartments on Rio Grande that were leased as of September 1, but they were unoccupied in the meantime. I offered Seton the use of three apartments for a period of two and a half months. I figured this would allow us time to assess the need for the kind of lodging Sister Mary Rose envisioned."

Those ten weeks saw the apartments filled to capacity, with a waiting list for other families who needed lodging. Clearly, the need for the proposed facility had been established. "When, as planned, my apartments were occupied on the first of September, we had to find a new place," says Dick. "Word of this Austin amenity had spread, and people were beginning to request lodging.

"So we rented a fourplex on a lot across the street from the hospital to use as a temporary space, even though it was already obvious that this two-story building was inadequate for the need we had uncovered. For one thing, a manager lived in one unit, which left only three apartments for patients' families. We needed quarters, and I strongly felt that they should be adjacent to, or at least within walking distance of, the hospital."

The problem was, there was no land near the hospital for building apartments.

"I kept mulling this over until one day when I was driving along 35th Street in front of the hospital," says Dick. "All at once the thought came to me: Aha! Why don't we build the housing on top of the parking garage?"

Excited, Dick called Page, Southerland & Page, the hospital's architects, who told him the idea wouldn't work because the parking garage was slated to be expanded. "Unfortunately, this news put me back at square one," he says. "But the architect *had* come up with one possible solution. He suggested using the metal Butler Building next to the main building."

Later that day, Dick returned to Seton and began driving slowly around the hospital complex, studying the aforementioned metal building. "After asking around, I learned that Seton used this area to store everything from beds to supplies to hospital records since the hospital didn't have off-site storage at the time."

Rathgeber began to envision taking the roof off, adding a second story, and then overhanging the second story about four feet on each side in order to improve the appearance. "We didn't want the building to look temporary or seem like an afterthought," he says. "But I could see what a great and convenient location this would be!"

Immediately Dick went to talk to Sister Mary Rose. "When I finished telling her my idea, I said, 'When we finish, I assure you the building will be good-looking! We are going to make a silk purse out of this sow's ear.' Sister was a lady of great faith, and she believed me. So we set about making it happen. Page, Southerland & Page donated their architectural services, and my company lined up a contractor for the construction. We put a blue awning on the building and an outside elevator, and it became very attractive."

Things went smoothly during this construction phase, but Rathgeber and the others did hit one snag during construction of the building. He explains, "The contractor made the tread on the steps a quarter-inch too high, and as a result the city building inspector red-tagged the project. When that happened, the contractor was ready to tear the steps out and start all over. I said, 'Let's go to the City of Austin Board of Adjustment. Since we have an elevator, this could really be considered a fire escape.'"

Dick took a nun with him when he was to make his presentation to the board. The sister insisted she was praying the whole time. "Over the strong objections of one city staff member, who opposed our request," says Dick, "the Board of Adjustment ruled in our favor. When the hearing was over, that city staffer glared at me from across the room. Later he passed me as he left the room. He gestured toward the nun and muttered, just loudly enough for me to hear him, 'You SOB, you wouldn't have won if you hadn't had her along.'

"I grinned and said, 'Whatever it takes.'"

This first building had a manager's quarters and fifteen

rooms, each with private bath. People were able to stay there at no charge, but guests were asked for a $10-$15 a night donation. "If they didn't have the money," says Dick, "they were treated as the hospital's guests. Most people did contribute, though, and this enabled the hospitality house to be self-supporting rather than a financial drain on the hospital."

Dick adds that the role of the Junior League was crucial in this process. "Under Carolyn Curtis's leadership, the Junior League raised money to help get the project moving," he says, "and in addition, the group's enthusiasm and support brought word of the facility to the attention of the wider community. In honor of their contribution, the facility was named the Seton League House."

As word of the Seton League House spread, demand for rooms increased. Within a year, the demand became so great that the hospital vacated the bottom of the building and added fifteen additional rooms with private baths. "My company at the time, Southwest Demolishing Company, did the contract work on that project, building partitions, adding bathrooms, and outfitting the building to accommodate twice as many families. We also contributed most of the money for the project," says Dick.

Additional expenses were raised through philanthropy. "Of course, Seton approached corporations and foundations, but they did something else that I thought was just ingenious. Since these hospitality houses are used mainly by people from outlying towns, it was essential from the start that those towns have a sense of ownership in the facility. To that end, Sister Gertrude Levy and Rick Resnik, who is head of development for Seton, spent months going from town to town in the Central Texas area, stopping at Catholic churches or visiting the mayor's office. They would show the town leaders photos and drawings of the facility and bring them into the loop on any planned expansion. Then they would ask each community for a $3,000 contribution in exchange for naming a room in the Seton League House after their community. Once the town agreed to that, Rick and Sister Gertrude would ask for $10,000 to cover expenses for building the room. So today the facility has rooms named for Round Rock, Georgetown, Dripping Springs, Marble Falls, Bastrop, Elgin. There are even rooms named for Houston and LaGrange. Lago Vista and Kingsland each have two rooms.

"This is what I mean by searching out your logical allies. The more people who feel ownership in a given project, the more successful it will be," Dick says.

The Seton League House was highly utilized, and Dick's involvement gave him clout with Sister Mary Rose and others in leadership at the hospital. "As soon as 'civilians,' or non-nuns, were invited to join the Seton Hospital board, I was asked to serve," he says, with a chuckle. "However, I have to say that I always noticed there was at least one more habit than suit in those meetings."

A few years later, the board decided that a brand-new forty-unit Seton League House should be constructed about a block from the hospital, on Lamar Boulevard between 34th and 35th Streets. That facility remains in operation today—and it is self-supporting!

# Abilene

After the proven success of the hospitality house in Austin, Dick began to recognize the need for a similar effort in other Texas communities. He had found this project highly satisfying, because he could see it was bringing comfort and a kind of relief to families in a time of great stress.

He explains how this work gradually spread. "After the need for these hospitality houses became clear to me, I realized I wanted to see more of them built. I was convinced that the Austin model could be replicated in other cities.

"However, I never believed in going into new territory without having a John the Baptist to prepare the way. To that end, I had some of the Seton people, including Rick Reznick and Gene Attal, who are Seton Development officers, contact Mike Waters, who was the CEO at Hendrick Medical Center in Abilene. At the same time, I asked Carolyn Curtis to contact the president of the Abilene Junior League and tell her what we were planning.

"I chose Abilene because it had a regional medical center. It's good to look for regional medical centers, because people from outlying areas come there for medical services, and those are the people who need this type of facility. Otherwise, small-town and rural people would have to drive back and forth at night, or they'd have to sleep at the hospital, or pay for a hotel room. Driving at night can be precarious, and of course they're often upset anyway, because their loved one is sick.

"We asked Hendrick's Mike Waters to set up a luncheon with key hospital people, members of their board, medical staff representatives, and members of the Abilene Junior League. I chartered a private plane to fly our contingent—which included Rick, Carolyn, a couple of other Austin Junior Leaguers, and me—out to Abilene.

"When we arrived at the meeting, I let my companions tell the story, but when they finished, I laid down my terms."

## DICK'S RULES FOR BUILDING
## A HOSPITALITY HOUSE

- First and foremost, the hospital has to furnish the land.
- The hospitality house needs to be immediately adjacent to the hospital.
- We bring in the hospital architects to work on the project, preferably pro bono.
- The hospital must make its fund-raising staff available to help raise the money.
- Also, the hospital must agree to go to the surrounding towns, to the Rotary, Kiwanis or Lions, whichever is the most prestigious in that town, and make a presentation to ask the town to sponsor a room. (Originally, the price tag for this was $10,000, but it has grown to $25,000.)
- Junior League must match funds. ($200,000 in 2007)
- Dick has to be allowed to approve the plans for the building.

If all the above requirements are met, Dick will provide matching funds.

At the Abilene meeting, which was the first one Dick oversaw after his Austin effort, things moved fast. Dick told them, "If you're prepared to go forward, I'll write you a check today for $125,000, and I expect the Abilene Junior League to match it." He remembers, "The Junior League accepted on the spot, and the hospital representatives were enthusiastic as well. They had to have a board meeting to approve the action, but even that day it was pretty clear what they were going to do. The deal was closed on the first call."

As a result, a hospitality facility was built fifty feet from Hendricks Hospital, on hospital property. Today the Hendrick League House describes itself this way on its Web site:

> *Welcome to Hendrick League House, your home away from home at Hendrick Medical Center. While your loved one is hospitalized at Hendrick Medical Center or using one of the outpatient facilities at Hendrick Medical Center, take advantage of this hotel-like atmosphere. Quality healthcare is first priority at Hendrick Medical Center, and part of that quality care is including the patient's family and friends in the recovery process. Located at 1910 Hickory, Hendrick League House is a convenient walk across the street to Hendrick Medical Center.*

## San Angelo

"This project actually came to me through an architect friend, a member of the old Pfluger family," Dick says, "who at that time was working as the hospital architect for a San Angelo hospital called St. Joseph's. My friend knew about what we'd done in Abilene, and as he studied the San Angelo community, he realized it needed a similar facility. He proposed the idea to the powers that be and asked me to get involved. I wrote a check for $150,000 or so, but I never really got involved in the fundraising. They had a going concern, so all they really needed from me was the grant. I went out for the dedication, though."

# Wichita Falls

"Wichita Falls had two competing hospitals. We started trying to do a hospitality house with one of them in the early 1980s, but negotiations dragged on through the 1980s, with the two hospitals fighting each other. Then, in 1989, the real estate and banking crash came, and I was no longer in a position to fund the hospital house

"Meanwhile, the two hospitals finally merged, and in driving through Wichita Falls with Sara on the way to Santa Fe sometime in the early 1990s, I recognized I had unfinished business there.

"I often joke that when I have my mind made up that something needs to be done, the first two 'no's' don't count. Well, I'd had my first two 'no's' in Wichita Falls, and now it was time to get down to business. I contacted the hospital again and I saw immediately that, in the interim since we had last spoken, the climate at the hospital had become much more receptive to the idea of a hospitality house.

"Management at Bethania Hospital, a Catholic hospital, agreed to move forward on building a hospitality house, using my model. They accepted my proposal of a $150,000 grant in return for naming the facility for my grandparents, Charles and Rose Rathgeber, who had come to Wichita Falls from Nebraska in the late 1890s. I thought this was a fitting tribute to my paternal grandparents, who began farming on 640 acres about five miles southeast of Wichita Falls. Rathgeber Road is on the state highway maps today.

"In the end, the Wichita Falls facility—the Charles and Rose Rathgeber Hospitality House—had twenty-six rooms with private baths, as well as a communal kitchen and living room. Heaviest use of the facility comes from Wilbarger County. Lockett is a small town twelve miles west of Vernon, a very small farming community on the highway to Crowell. I graduated from Lockett High School in 1950, with a class of twenty-five students. I had the highest average of the boys. I always said there were twenty-five people in my class, but when Sara and I went to my fiftieth high school reunion, she looked at the yearbook and counted only eighteen.

"When we went to that reunion, we stayed at the Rathgeber House and drove over to Vernon for the reunion. The school I went to is extinct. Now the kids from my old stomping ground are bussed into Vernon.

"A young woman named Kim Tomlinson has been the manager of the Rathgeber House since its inception. She joined the National Association of Hospitality Houses and soon became a member of its national advisory board. She has done a fantastic job of running the house, and in only six years of operation she has built up an operating surplus of more than $400,000. She uses innovative approaches to fund-raising. For one thing, the house isn't subsidized by the hospital, so Kim sells sponsorships. Sponsors are recognized on a banner displayed in front of the house. Kim also keeps in touch with former guest residents, and she publishes a list of needs, such as toilet paper, laundry detergent, and cleaning supplies. Supporters then contribute those items and thus protect the house's bottom line. She is a really hard worker, and highly competent."

## Shreveport

"Sara has an aunt in Shreveport who is the last of a dying breed. She was a Leap Year baby, and for her eightieth birthday, she celebrated turning twenty with a big birthday party. Sara and I drove over to Shreveport to attend. At the party, I met some Shreveport Junior League members, and you can imagine the course our conversation took. I asked them whether they had a hospitality house in Shreveport.

"'No,' one young woman said, 'but we have been trying to get one for three years. We think we have finally got something lined up.'

"I probed for details and learned that one of the Methodist churches there had a vacant house that they were going to allow to be used as a hospitality house until the church needed the property for its own use.

"'How far is this house from the hospital?' I asked.

"'About ten blocks,' replied one young woman.

"No, no. This was in violation of one of my basic precepts that the hospitality house should be located within one hundred feet of at least one of the hospital's entrances. As I explained all this, I could feel myself being pulled into the business of helping Shreveport build a hospitality house that would really work. I have never been able to resist addressing a need that is placed right in front of me this way. If a glaring need is right in my path, and I have the resources and skills to help, how can I walk around it? Shreveport is not my home, and Louisiana isn't my state. Surely there were enough towns in Texas that needed my services. But I blundered on, because Shreveport was placed before me.

"I told the young women what I was doing in Austin and Abilene, and they asked if they could take me around the next morning and show me what they were planning to do. Shreveport's Schumpert Medical Center is a huge Catholic institution. The Leaguers drove me around and showed me their proposed location. I was completely unimpressed.

"I kept having them drive me around the hospital, and I would say, 'Who owns this land?'

"'Oh, that belongs to the hospital,' they would answer.

"While parked outside the Schumpert Hospital, I asked my companions, 'Who is in charge around here?'

"'A little Irish nun named Sister Agnesita runs things here, and she is tough as nails,' they told me.

"'Let's go see her,' I exclaimed.

"Fortunately Sister Agnesita was in, and I explained to her what I was doing elsewhere, and what I would like to do here in Shreveport. I said, 'I would like to name the hospitality house for Sara's grandfather, James McDade, who was a prominent local civic leader.'

"Later I said, 'Now, Sister Agnesita, you do understand that this proposition operates on the Golden Rule.'

"'Vat's that?' she asked.

"'Them that's got the gold makes the rules,' I replied.

"She nearly fell out of her chair laughing, and I knew I had won her over.

"She had me come back three weeks later, and when I did, it was to a full press conference with the television cameras and reporters from the *Shreveport Times*. During the press conference, Sister Agnesita proudly announced the plans for building the McDade Hospitality House.

"I love dealing with Catholic nuns, because they don't bother with democracy."

# Corpus Christi

"Spohn Hospital system in Corpus Christi is the largest in the area. In the mid-1980s, it was run by Sister Kathleen, a very progressive nun who dressed in civilian clothes. She was receptive to the idea of a hospitality house. To build it, though, a building needed to be demolished, which was about a $25,000 project. Well, I had an Austin architect friend name Jim Polkinghorn, who was doing some work in Corpus at the time. He agreed to do most of the architectural work on the project, pro bono. I paid for engineering, some of the inspections, and other matters Polkinghorn could not do himself.

"I had asked that the house be named for my great-grandfather Otto Kieschnick, who had been a pioneer settler of the nearby town of Bishop.

"Sister Kathleen had agreed to my request, but as the time approached for the groundbreaking, she kept talking about how hard Kieschnick was to spell and to pronounce. I talked to my relatives, and they assured me they wanted the building to be called the Kieschnick House.

"It was obvious to me what Sister Kathleen had in mind, so I sat down and wrote her a letter in which I said that I had never put my proposal in writing, and that, in fact, I did not have one proposal, but two. The first proposal was that my company would do the $25,000 site-clearing job and pay out-of-pocket expenses for the architect. She could call the facility anything she wanted to. The second proposal, however, included all of the above plus $125,000, in which case the facility would be named the Kieschnick House.

"The Kieschnick House in Corpus Christi is a fine twenty-room facility with private baths for all rooms. In the living room hangs a portrait of my great-grandfather Otto Kieschnick holding my mother, Esther Kieschnick Rathgeber, who was his oldest grandchild and was nine months old at the time the picture was painted."

# Albuquerque

"In Albuquerque, it became very apparent why it was crucial to have architectural approval for a hospitality house. The University of New Mexico Medical Center in Albuquerque had a tremendous need for a hospitality house, because they treated so many patients from all over with high-dose radiation. At the time, we had a condo in Santa Fe, and we went through Albuquerque quite often, since that was where we landed when we flew in.

"One time when I was there, I approached the hospital fund-raising staff, and I learned they had started plans for a hospitality house. In fact, they had drawn final plans. Albuquerque's leading architect had donated the plan, and his wife was on the board of the hospitality house. They were trying to raise money to move forward. I got to know some of the people who were involved, and they showed me the plans. I saw plans for a magnificent building, with spacious living rooms, but only eight units for guests.

"Bryan Lewis is an architect friend of mine. He took the footprint of the original plan and he was able to design forty guest rooms, each with bath, and still leave adequate space for a living room and kitchen.

"Since I was the out-of-town expert, I was able to get the board out of a very prickly situation by pointing out what they really needed. Casa Esperanza is a beautiful hospitality house, but its construction coincided with the crash of 1989, so I was unable to help financially. Even so, I thought the advice I gave them was of even greater value."

# Amarillo

At the 2002 Christmas Affair, the main Austin Junior League fund-raiser, Dick struck up a conversation with a young woman he hadn't met before. "She was a very nice young lady named Suzie O'Brien," Dick recalls, "and I learned she was from Amarillo. I asked her whether there was a hospitality house in her town, and she said no. I started my pitch, telling her exactly what a League House is, and how it benefits the community."

Ms. O'Brien's enthusiasm was such that she went home and started talking up the idea to her cohorts. Then the group invited Dick to visit. "In December 2002, I flew out to Amarillo and made a presentation to the entire Junior League," he says, "and I included my usual offer of a matching challenge grant. In response, the Junior League there appointed a committee, to be headed by Stacey Harwell. In September 2003, the League voted to proceed, naming Stacey and Lori Henke as co-chairs to begin fund-raising."

Over the following five years, the Amarillo Junior League raised nearly its entire share of the money. Dick says, "The Amarillo League House is scheduled to break ground in October 2008. My deal with them is that they get $50,000 each year, until a total of $200,000 is reached. They'll match that amount for a total of $400,000, but of course the hospitality house will be a $3.4 million project when completed. Most of the remaining money has been raised from foundations, grants, and the community."

When completed, the facility will be situated in the Harrington Medical Center, and it will include thirty guest units. Concludes Dick, "I want to be sure each hospitality house becomes a reality, so I don't write the first check until the slab is poured."

## Coming Soon: Beaumont

Rathgeber got to know attorney Wayne Reaud when Reaud provided $1 million to the Austin Children's Shelter, to be used in building the administration building. Soon after, the two men started talking about helping Beaumont secure a hospitality house. "Initially, Wayne thought about trying to do one in Lubbock because he went to law school at Texas Tech," Dick says, "but then he learned that the Lubbock house was to be used exclusively for cancer patients. He wanted a more inclusive place."

With St. Elizabeth's Hospital in Beaumont, Reaud started working on plans for an eighteen-room hospitality house. Dick says, "It was agreed that we would also assist with a generous donation. It really pays to get to know somebody like Wayne Reaud, because once he decides to do something he can make it happen. At the present time, plans are in the final stages, and bids are being taken for a hospitality house in Beaumont."

# Bring Opposing Sides to the Table

In 2003, the capital of Texas was roiling with a controversy that had it all: power, religion, politics, little children, class, health, and, if not sex, at least reproductive rights. At the center of the storm was the chronically overcrowded Brackenridge Hospital, which had long been situated on Interstate 35 in central Austin. Home to both the children's hospital and the regional trauma center, Brackenridge was owned by the city and managed by the Seton Family of Hospitals, a Catholic health-care network whose parent company is Ascencion Health, the largest not-for-profit health system in the United States. With a network of more than seventy-five health-care facilities in twenty states and the District of Columbia, Ascension employs more than 100,000 people. The company is headquartered in St. Louis, Missouri.

An organization of that size is like a huge ocean liner: once it's heading in a certain direction, it's just too big to change course. Even so, when Seton decided to move the children's hospital to a site far north of the urban center, everybody in town had an opinion, none of them positive.

"Doctors were mad. City officials were mad. Everybody was mad," observes Rathgeber, who was watching from the sidelines as events unfolded. "It was a mess."

As interest groups formed and rumors mushroomed, people lined up in camps. The brouhaha continued to gain momentum, simply because it affected the lives of so many people in Austin. The more Rathgeber read about the commotion and heard on the street about how up in arms everyone was about it, the more determined he became to help solve the problem.

"Seton was taking a real pounding in the press at that time," he recalls. "I knew the people at Seton. I'd served on its board of directors for a few years, and I helped bring together Seton, the Austin Junior League, and others to establish a hospitality house. Seton did a lot of good in the community, so it was a shame to see the hospital vilified. But at the same time, moving so far away from downtown *did* seem to be a mistake."

Rathgeber was also well acquainted with Austin's city manager, Toby Futrell, who at that time was dealing with a furious city council, a confused populace, and a hospital that was dead set on moving. Rathgeber had worked with Futrell and the city on several large development projects, and she had confidence in his integrity. Because Dick had earned credibility with Futrell over the years, she was ready to listen to him in the matter of the children's hospital.

With this fray as with all others, of course, there's a backstory. "In the first place, it's unusual for a hospital to be owned by a city," Futrell explains. "Public hospitals are typically owned by counties. However, about a hundred years ago, Austin got into a dispute with Travis County over management of the hospital, and the county walked away. So, early in the twentieth century, the City of Austin found itself proud owner of a hospital that served more than ten surrounding counties, and consequently in charge of a medical lifeline for all of Central Texas."

Austin city officials managed to run the hospital for decades, but it was really too much for them, and by 1994 they'd lost $50 million. "Hospitals don't blend easily into a city's budget," Futrell says, "and a trauma center is a particular drain on the economy."

So it seemed propitious back in October 1995 when Seton stepped in with an offer to manage Brackenridge. Under the agreement, the City of Austin would retain ownership of the hospital, but the lease for operations and maintenance would be Seton's. It was a deal that, in effect, gave Ascension long-term ownership of Brackenridge.

"What Seton and Ascension got in the deal was a very profitable children's hospital and a very unprofitable trauma center," Futrell says. "Trauma centers are set up for emergencies, and they can't turn people away, so invariably they lose money. Trauma is never profitable. A children's hospital, by contrast, is typically very profitable."

The arrangement between the city and Seton was backed by a $5 million severance fee. That is, if either partner walked away from the deal, that partner would have to pay $5 million to the other partner. This contract continued for ten or so years, during which time the hospital broke even. However, Austin's population was soaring during those years, and as it did, Brackenridge began to bulge with sick kids. The situation was intolerable, and everyone agreed something had to be done.

That's when Seton announced that Ascension, as the hospital's parent company, was moving the children's hospital to far north Austin. At the same time, Seton announced that its management would be taking over ownership of the hospital.

And with that, all hell broke loose.

People worried that Seton would abandon the trauma center and the newer hospital-within-a-hospital for women at Brackenridge, but Seton CEO Charles Barnett says that was never the plan. "We were committed to the city long-term. Our lease agreement was a thirty-year plus a thirty-year agreement, and we had even signed an extension on that. We expected to operate Brackenridge forever. We weren't going to abandon the trauma center."

However, hospital management's reassurances did little to soothe an anxious public, which also fretted over local women's access to reproductive services. As a Catholic system, Seton is on record as opposing abortion and most forms of birth control. As long as the city was in charge, the public felt confident that a way would be found to offer these services to women. But if the hospital fell under Catholic ownership, what would happen to women's services?

City officials saw Seton's decision as arbitrary. "By dividing the trauma center from the children's facilities," explains Futrell, "the lease would stay in place, but Seton was moving the only thing that made any money. Plus, the children's hospital wouldn't be a publicly owned hospital anymore."

Adding to the complexity of the issue was the fact that Austin is a city whose population is divided into the west side, which is prosperous, and the east side, whose residents, generally speaking, rank lower on the socioeconomic scale. What was going to happen to the children on the east side? How would they even get to the hospital now?

"We tried to stop Seton from moving out of reach of so many people," Futrell says. "We offered them all kinds of tracts closer in, near the existing hospital, but they wouldn't budge. Their land had been purchased. Their plans were laid. So, great! The trauma center would remain in place at Brackenridge, and the city would keep the money drain while the only real asset bailed out."

Add to that the will of the medical profession itself. "The doctors didn't want to go north, so they organized around this issue, and they were the wrath of God itself," Futrell says.

Wave after wave of protest erupted. "Why not stay central?" people demanded. In newspaper articles, letters to the editor, and water cooler conversations, it was suggested that Seton consider moving to the Mueller Airport redevelopment site. After Austin Bergstrom Airport opened in 1999, the centrally located Mueller, a huge tract of land, sat untouched for years while the city decided what to do with it. Located a few miles north of Brackenridge on Interstate 35, the site was wide open, close in, ideal.

But with overcrowding at Brackenridge reaching the crisis stage, Ascension didn't want to jump through municipal hoops, or engage with neighborhood politics. Says Seton CEO Charles Barnett, "We'd always looked at the Mueller site as preferred, but the mayor at that time, Gus Garcia, said it couldn't be available in time to open when we wanted to open."

Catellus, a development company headquartered in San Francisco, had landed the Mueller project and put a young up-and-comer named Greg Weaver in charge. The city was in the middle of negotiations with Catellus, and nobody wanted to be forced to rework the deal. In any case, there was no room in Mueller's plans for a hospital, children's or otherwise.

Toby Futrell says, "It's true the Mueller plan as it then stood didn't leave a spare inch for a hospital. In his defense, Barnett thought he would be in the middle of an intense re-thinking of the whole Mueller plan if he agreed to build there. This could involve negotiations that would ensnarl things for months or years. So we made other suggestions for locations, all close to the city center. Every time Seton would offer objections to a tract we had submitted, we would counter with another alternative. But hospital man-agement was completely dug in. They were building at Palmer and I-35, and that was that. At City Hall, we were angry. We started thinking of litigation."

"Around town, this situation was on everybody's mind, and the more I talked to people about it," remembers Dick Rathgeber, "the more I wondered what solution could ever be reached. I didn't have any power in the situation, but I do like to find solutions, and this was a doozie of a problem."

He decided to jump in. He knew Greg Weaver. In fact, Rathgeber had bid on the Mueller project himself, and Catellus had beaten him out. This, however, did nothing to put an end to Rathgeber's interest in what happened there.

"Here are the facts," Dick says. "The city came up with a plan for Mueller, working with all these neighborhoods and citizen groups. You can't make a cohesive plan working by committee. At that time there was a glut of vacant down-town office space. The committee's plan called for five mil-lion square feet of office space—the equivalent of all the of-fice space that had been built downtown and was now standing empty."

Rathgeber's group had submitted an incomplete bid for the Mueller job, because Dick and his partners did not feel that the plan as designed was financially feasible. In fact, they doubted that financing would be available for office space in a Class B location—which Mueller was, since it was both far from the urban center and east of I-35. Complications such as these had slowed the deal, which at the time of this meeting had not been inked between the city and Catellus.

Rathgeber had bought a sixteen-acre plot of ground adjacent to the Mueller site that same year, and while the children's hospital controversy raged on, he was mulling over some long-term philanthropic plans for that land. He asked Greg Weaver about the possibility of moving the hospital to Mueller. Weaver was highly skeptical, but he agreed to come to a meeting about it.

Of course, from his time on the Seton board, Rathgeber also knew Seton CEO Charles Barnett, so he approached Barnett about building the hospital at Mueller. He got the same answers everyone else had. There were too many hoops to jump through. It would take too long—at least two years—before construction could begin on the hospital. Seton wanted to be in place and operational by August 2007. And Austin couldn't wait two years, because sick children were sleeping in the halls at Brackenridge.

Around that time, Charles Barnett asked Dick to lunch with the new CEO of the children's hospital, Bob Bonar. Bonar had just arrived in Austin from Virginia, and as soon as he got to town he realized he was on the hot seat. "I was really excited about this opportunity," says Bonar. "Austin's children's hospital was to be a Brownfield Project, which meant that we would be designing and building the facility from the ground up. Also, it was going to be the first LEED (Leadership in Environment Energy and Design) hospital in the world. This is a designation by the U.S. Green Building Council, awarded because the design was on the cutting edge of environmentally responsible hospital design. When I was hired, I was told that teams would be coming in from as far away as Australia and Russia to study our innovations. It's not very often that you get an opportunity like this."

He chuckles. "But when I arrived in Austin, it didn't take me long to figure out I'd landed in the eye of a big storm. I started asking myself why I'd left Virginia. I was happy there, and the board liked me there—while here in Austin, controversy swirled all around me.

"Pat Hayes was Seton CEO at the time, and Charles Barnett was president and CEO of all Ascencion's southern hospitals. Therefore, while all this was going on, Charles had been pulled away to oversee the larger operation. Even so, he was around enough to be sure that I met all the movers and shakers in town."

To this end, Barnett had arranged for Bob to meet Dick Rathgeber for lunch at the Headliners Club, a fifty-year-old private club in downtown Austin. Situated atop the Chase Tower, the Headliners Club has long been the site of choice for parties, receptions, and dinners for its members, who enjoy exquisite food and an unparalleled view of Austin. Members include governors and former governors of the state, Nobel laureates, philanthropists, actors, journalists, and other figures of statewide and national prominence.

"About the time we met for lunch, there were articles, letters to the editor, and editorials blasting Seton for moving so far out," Rathgeber recalls.

Bonar says Rathgeber addressed the situation head-on that day. "His exact words were, 'You people are really taking a pounding in the press, aren't you? If I could get the city to collaborate on land at Mueller, and do it on your schedule, how soon could you get started?'"

This was a preposterous idea, but Charles Barnett knew Dick, so he replied cautiously that Mueller was the obvious first choice for everybody, including Seton, and that of course they could start right away under the circumstances Dick proposed. "But we can't wait," Barnett warned. "Children are stacked on top of each other at Brackenridge, and we want to open the doors of the new facility by August 2007."

That date was less than four years away.

Rathgeber said, "Just let me see what I can do."

Dick called a meeting of the key players. Toby Futrell and the city were skeptical, because Seton had been so stubborn and unbending. Greg Weaver of Catellus was reluctant to come, because he was in the middle of negotiating his agreement with the city. And Seton didn't want to come because the hospital had a mission, and a plan for realizing it. Seton's management didn't want to be derailed at this point. Furthermore, hospital representatives feared the city would have lawyers there.

"There won't be any lawyers present," Dick promised. "We're just going to get together and see if we can come to an understanding."

"No lawyers?" asked Charles Barnett.

"No lawyers. I'll wear a striped shirt and carry a whistle, and if anybody gets out of hand, I'll throw the flag," said Dick.

Eventually all the officials from the city, the hospital, and Catellus agreed to meet—but nobody had much hope that things would work out. After all, that big municipal ocean liner had set out for a particular shore, and it wasn't about to change course.

THE NIGHT BEFORE THE MEETING, Rathgeber called Mary Ann Roser, a reporter for the *Austin American-Statesman* whose beat was health and the health-care industry. He told her that he had a story for her, but that she had to promise not to release it until he gave the word. Then he filled her in on the planned meeting. He supplied all the details about who would be at the sit-down and what he thought could be accomplished. And he made her promise to hold the story until he could see how it would come out.

ON THE DAY OF THE MEETING, Dick arrived at City Hall early and double-checked to be sure the room was ready. Present were Toby Futrell and Austin CFO John Stephens for the city, as well as Charles Barnett, Bob Bonar, and Travis Froelich, Seton's communications director, for the hospital. Catellus was represented by a reluctant and skeptical Greg Weaver. No lawyers were present.

Rathgeber remembers the meeting well. People were lined up on either side of a table and everyone was wary. "I started by asking each side what its greatest fear was. Toby admitted the city was afraid that Seton could essentially buy them out for $5 million and leave them holding the bag with the trauma center. Seton, meanwhile, worried that a renegade city council could be elected, and it would vote in another operator for the children's hospital. All they'd have to do to make that happen was to pay $5 million to Seton. Then they could walk away."

To Dick, the first step toward an agreement was clear. "Friends, the divorce settlement needs to go up," he said to the group, and it was subsequently decided that the separation fee would increase to $50 million. "At that point," Rathgeber says, "if either side wanted to break the deal, they'd have to pay the other that amount. That decided, our conversation got to the point."

Toby Futrell agrees that the money helped. "Events had occurred in a way that added up to the perfect storm," she says. "With the $50 million ante, we knew Seton wouldn't just walk away. It was enough to firm up the commitment, put the financial info on the table, and alleviate some of the city's and the public's fears."

"I never had to throw the flag at the meeting," Rathgeber reports. "Peace and love prevailed. When people who are at odds talk to each other, and each side listens to the other, solutions *do* come about."

Before the meeting adjourned, Dick alerted Futrell and Charles Barnett that reporter Mary Ann Roser would be calling them. "I urge you to talk to her and, in fact, I'd like to give her your cell phone numbers to make it easier for her to reach you," he said.

"When I left the meeting, I knew it was going to work out for the hospital to move. Unless Catellus dug in, that is—and it was clear that the hospital could be the engine that would drive the whole Mueller project.

"Even so, it took a lot of good faith on the part of the city, Catellus, and the hospital, because plans hadn't been finalized. Each side had to trust the others to do exactly what was agreed in that private meeting. Things could have imploded, except that there was genuine good faith among the players. Everyone wanted what was best for the city."

Looking back, Charles Barnett says, "Knowing Dick's persuasiveness, I wasn't really worried. I have a lot of trust and confidence in Dick, and when he said he thought the city would accelerate the sale, I believed him. I know he delivers when he commits. Besides, Dick was in a good position to broker this agreement. People trust Dick. He had credibility with the city because he had demonstrated his commitment."

Bob Bonar agrees. "I could see that Dick was savvy about business, and also connected to people in the community. For these reasons, he had the influence to be an opinion shaper. Because he had access to people, he could do back-channel negotiations."

Toby Futrell says, "Dick was a key player in this deal. He brought all sides together. In my view, there were three legs of the stool: Dick, the outraged doctors, and a number of key Austinites who had put a lot of money into Seton and who might have stopped their support if we hadn't come to a satisfactory solution."

Today, the factions all speak warmly of one another. Says Seton's Barnett, "I applaud Toby Futrell, because she agreed to give us the contract before the city had a firm contract with Catellus. The truth is, we had always looked at the Mueller site as preferred, but we were assured the land couldn't be available in time to open when we hoped, because Catellus wasn't even finished with its contract. It was only logical that the city would have a contract and a plan for developing Mueller before they could make land available for a hospital, but thanks to that meeting, special arrangements enabled Catellus to sell the land to us immediately. We then moved as fast as we could, and we beat our own deadline."

The Michael and Susan Dell Foundation made a challenge grant of $25 million, and today the hospital has raised $85 million. With the exception of the University of Texas, this is the largest capital campaign in Central Texas history.

In July 2007, a month ahead of schedule, Austin's new children's hospital opened its doors.

Concludes Rathgeber, "This was a complicated deal, but it was a complicated deal with a simple answer."

---

## A Perfect Union: Mueller, Seton hospital

*Austin American-Statesman* editorial

Sunday, February 2, 2003

Children's Hospital needs a new home. The Mueller redevelopment project needs an engine. We hope there is a marriage in the making.

It's true the courtship has been stormy. But remaining obstacles can be overcome if both sides are willing to compromise. If they do, children and taxpayers will be better for it.

Seton Healthcare Network, which has proposed to build a new children's hospital in far North Austin, initially rebuffed overtures by the city to build on the site of the former Robert Mueller Municipal Airport. Seton purchased land on Parmer Lane and Interstate 35 for that hospital. (Seton now manages the city-owned Children's Hospital.) The *American-Statesman*'s Mary Ann Roser reported that Seton now is pursuing the Mueller site as a home for its planned hospital. It's hardly a done deal, though.

A major question to be resolved is whether Seton or the city would own the hospital. Seton says it should own the new children's hospital because it's investing the money to

(Continued on next page)

build it. The city has resisted that because it would lose ownership of its one profitable hospital, Children's.

## Location important

The Mueller site has a lot to offer Seton, including location, location, location. The Mueller site in Central Austin is preferable to Seton's North Austin site.

If Seton goes ahead with its plans for a private children's hospital, trauma services would remain at city-owned Brackenridge in downtown Austin. (Seton also manages Brackenridge.) That means doctors and pediatric surgeons would work at two locations. The commute to the North Austin location would take 20 to 40 minutes, depending on traffic. By contrast, it's a 10-minute hop to the Mueller site from Children's Hospital. No wonder Children's doctors cheered when they heard Mueller might be their new home.

Seton has a lot to offer Mueller, which desperately needs a catalyst to drive its $1 billion redevelopment.

On these pages, we endorsed the Mueller master plan crafted by city officials and Mueller neighborhoods that would transform the airport's rubble and grassy fields into a showplace neighborhood with housing for 10,000 people, a grocery store, shops, parks and offices.

That was nearly three years ago, and still no dirt has been turned. If the city and its master developer, Catellus Commercial Group of San Francisco, pull it off, it would be a boon for taxpayers and residents looking for affordable housing near downtown.

Construction is supposed to start late this year or in

(Continued on next page)

2004. But we've grown concerned about the progress of this ambitious project, which was approved in better economic times. Then, downtown office space was pricey and scarce; initial public offerings were in the air; sales taxes were growing; the city's budget was in the black; and job growth was a healthy 5.9 percent.

The Mueller site was attractive to businesses planning expansions or residents who wanted an affordable home or apartment close to downtown.

Fast forward to 2003. Austin has a glut in downtown office space; apartment and home prices have declined; sales taxes are shrinking and the city budget is $58 million in the red. (And let's not talk about jobs that disappeared in the past year.) Mueller's beauty has faded.

All of those are reasons why a marriage between Mueller and Seton is a good match. The planned children's hospital generally fits within the scheme of the Mueller master plan. The $175 million facility and accompanying $25 million physicians' building would give the project a financial infusion and anchor tenant. At this point, Mueller has few suitors who can bring such a dowry to the table.

Moving Seton's hospital to the Mueller site also would generate potential home buyers and renters for the houses and apartments that will be built there.

### Talks in action

We thank Austin developer and philanthropist Dick Rathgeber, who helped bring both sides back to the bargaining table. City Manager Toby Futrell said Seton and the city are negotiating, and things look "promising." She acknowl-

(Continued on next page)

edged hurdles and risks: The deal would have to win approval from the City Council, Catellus and Mueller-area neighborhoods.

Mueller's redevelopment also could suffer a setback if the economy again contracts. And there is the threat by state Rep. Ron Wilson, D-Houston, who has filed a bill to re-open Mueller as a general aviation airport. Wilson might want to reconsider his legislation, given that Mueller's terminals have been demolished and sections of its runways dug up. By joining Seton and Mueller, we could put an end to Wilson's brazen grab for turf that he wants to spare his chums who make the longer commute from the Austin-Bergstrom International Airport in Del Valle. Planning for the wedding reception might be premature, but we at least ought to work up the guest list for this union.

# Maximize Your Philanthropic Return on Investment (ROI)

The effective philanthropist, according to Dick, is the one who seeks the greatest return on each dollar contributed. In other words, before giving to a cause, it's wise to study the overall effect of the program or service. He says, "The first thing I consider in deciding whether to support a project is how many people can be helped, how efficiently, with how much dignity for the recipients. And, of course, at what cost?"

Dick's second consideration has two parts: "Is somebody else helping the group? And is the group helping itself?"

Obviously, one contributor can't single-handedly support a program, so it's important for any nonprofit to seek funding from a variety of sources. "Like most givers, I want to know that the organization is shaking all the trees for funding," Dick says. "The more people who are motivated to get involved, the more successful the organization will be."

So a philanthropist should do what he or she can to increase the return on investment. How?

Following are a few examples of programs to which Rathgeber has contributed, all of which have wide-ranging payoffs—meaning the dollars he contributed have multiplied exponentially.

## The Chapel at the Del Valle Jail

"Bishop John McCarthy was the Catholic bishop in the 1990s," Dick says, "and he was very interested in the poor of all shapes and varieties. The bishop has a heart of gold, and when he was in office, he accomplished many charitable endeavors. One thing he especially hoped to bring about was the building of a chapel for the inmates at the Del Valle jail. To that end, he had a Catholic deacon working for him, and this deacon was responsible for going to all the churches in town, asking for donations for the chapel after services. On a good day, he would collect between $200 and $300.

"One day I was in conversation with Bishop McCarthy, and we decided to enlist the aid of Margo Frazier, the Travis County sheriff at that time. It had come to our attention that she had a commissary jail fund that had just about enough money in it to finance one-third of the chapel cost. Bishop McCarthy and I agreed to take responsibility for the remaining two-thirds, and we set about scheduling a fund-raising luncheon. The cost to build this chapel would be much less than usual because the jail inmates would contribute all the labor, including rock work, painting, and laying the floor covering.

"We scheduled the fund-raising luncheon for about twenty-five civic leaders at the Headliners Club. At the luncheon, Bishop McCarthy made a stirring appeal, outlining the need for funds and the benefits that would derive from a jail chapel. At the end of the luncheon, John Selman, a leading Austin attorney, asked if we were going to have a fund-raiser. 'Selman,' I replied, 'we just did.'

"Within a year, the beautiful white cut-limestone chapel and recreation room had been finished. We all hoped that this building would serve as inspiration and beacon of hope to all who worshiped there."

## Lady Bird Johnson and the Wildflower Center

Having worked with Carolyn Curtis on the Seton League House and other League Houses, Dick could hardly turn down an invitation to have lunch with her and David Northington, the director of the Wildflower Center. "David and Carolyn were very concerned about how the center would continue to operate after Mrs. Johnson was no longer able to take a leading role in fund-raising," Dick says. "They were looking for ideas, and they had thought about selling T-shirts or packages of wildflower seeds to raise money. I said, 'No, you need big money. You need about a $15 million endowment.' I told them Mrs. Johnson needed to get board members and friends, such as David Rockefeller, who was then on the board, to contribute. 'But,' I added, 'Mrs. Johnson will need to give the first million.'

"They responded almost in unison, 'Oh, Dick, we can't ask her to do that.' I replied that I would approach her, but I wasn't going to do so as a supplicant. I told them that the meeting needed to take place at a neutral site."

Carolyn and David set up the meeting at the Headliners Club (where else?), and Dick showed up with a plan. "I outlined the need for big contributions," he explains, "and I put heavy emphasis on the fact that Mrs. Johnson would need to give the first million dollars. 'Oh,' she said in her genteel Southern drawl, 'I just don't think I could ask my friends to do something like that.'

"'But Mrs. Johnson,' I said, 'I just asked *you* for a million dollars.' She replied, 'But you're so self-assured!' I found it amusing that a former First Lady thought that a country preacher's son could do something with ease that she couldn't bring herself to do. Obviously, however, she found a way, because the Wildflower Center was able to raise a sizable endowment for its continued support."

## People's Community Clinic

For years, Austin's tiny Congregational church, located at San Antonio and 23rd Street near the U.T. Drag, housed People's Community Clinic, a medical clinic for homeless people. However, when the Americans with Disabilities Act (ADA) was passed in 1990, the clinic learned that it was going to lose all government funding. The reason? Its facility was on three floors, and some clients couldn't climb the stairs.

At the time, the clinic was serving hundreds of impoverished Austinites, including scores of pregnant women living at or below the poverty line. Everyone agreed the clinic needed to stay open. Yet it operated on a shoestring and certainly couldn't afford to bring the church up to ADA code. The clinic was at a crossroads.

The folks at People's had first contacted Dick for advice the previous year, in 1989, because they knew of his effectiveness in getting a site for the downtown Salvation Army homeless shelter.

"I agreed to visit with Roseanna Szilak, then director of the People's Clinic," Dick said, "as well as a few interested board members who wanted me to help them figure out how to move from the Congregational church."

As he spent time with the people in charge of People's Community Clinic, Rathgeber became increasingly confident that People's was a worthy cause. Very soon, he pledged $50,000, even though, along with so many businesspeople in Austin, his financial situation was precarious. He recalls, "People's call had come at a very bad time for me. I was trying to work my way out from under the debacle of that real estate crash, in which I had recently lost nine-tenths of my net worth. So I made that pledge strictly on faith, without a clue as to where the money would come from, and the reason I did is that I could see how many people were served by the clinic. People's has 60,000 to 70,000 individual patient visits every year—and they serve those clients on a sliding scale. Patients pay only what they can afford to pay."

Several factors enter into Rathgeber's decision to help an organization financially. Primary among these is how the organization treats the people it serves. "It's very important to me that services be delivered in a way that allows recipients to retain their dignity," he says. "And, secondly, I want to see real bang for the buck. The business side of philanthropy dictates that a person is not able to help everybody who needs help. But if a philanthropist does his homework, he can be sure his dollars will stretch."

The immediate concern for the People's Clinic, though, was the question of where to locate. Dick and the clinic management studied their options. At first, they thought about moving to the Salvation Army building at 501 East 8th Street, but it was ultimately decided that was not a good idea. For one thing, the Salvation Army didn't have room.

"They looked at several pieces of property before eventually deciding on the present location, at 30½ and I-35, right across from St. David's Hospital. The building had been an obstetrics and gynecology clinic whose doctors had moved to a new location.

"By coincidence, on the day I first visited, vandals had broken in and turned on the water, stopped up the sinks, and ruined all the flooring. So the clinic's problems had already compounded, even before I arrived. We opened the door, and water ran out over our feet. We saw that the whole building was flooded with three or four inches of water. Also, the carpet was soggy and smelled bad."

Rathgeber recalls that when Roseanna saw the flooding, her face just fell. "Hey, don't worry," Dick told her. "You're a lucky lady. Now you're going to get all new carpet!"

Yet once again the clinic came up against daunting ADA standards: the bathrooms in the building didn't meet government specifications for the disabled. The clinic had already signed a lease for the building, so they were cornered. Roseanna contacted Dick to make the necessary modifications to the restrooms.

"I asked to read the lease, and when I did, I saw it named the tenant as responsible for leaks, air-conditioning, and all upkeep of the property. This didn't seem fair to me. In the first place, the AC was old. I persuaded the owners to change the lease, take care of maintenance, and also to give the clinic two months' free rent to compensate for its modifying the restrooms and lighting the parking lot. I agreed to do that work, but insisted the clinic pay for supplies, which totaled $7,500, a fairly significant amount for them. As I said earlier, I feel strongly that any nonprofit should do all it can."

Dick took People's $7,500, completed all the repairs and lighting, and still had a little money left over for paint.

Unfortunately, soon after the facility was habitable, Rathgeber began to comprehend the full scope of the needs there. "In addition to a suitable building, which they finally had, the clinic needed money for rent, utilities, medication, salaries, and uncounted other expenses. Now, I don't like raising funds for operating expenses, because I think that promotes dependency. I try to help worthy organizations out of the ditch, and then I leave them alone to do their work. I don't join the board or try to direct the organization in any way. I just move on to the next project. I enjoy chasing the deal, and if I can do that in behalf of a good cause, so much the better."

However, he wasn't yet ready to move on from the People's Community Clinic. As he considered the good work the clinic was doing, Dick began to see the organization's need for permanence. "It seemed to me the clinic's first need was to own and control its own building," he says. "I proposed this, and the board of directors agreed. Then they agreed to let me make it happen."

He decided to start a capital campaign to help raise the money People's needed to buy, and then renovate, the building. "At that time, the building was still owned by the doctors who had worked there, so I approached them first," he says. "After several conversations, I was able to negotiate a bargain sale for the clinic: no money down, a no-liability note, and the same $3,750-a-month rent People's had already been paying. This arrangement was attractive to the doctors because it freed them of the maintenance headaches always associated with owning a good-sized, publicly used building. Also, it got the clinic building off the tax roll, since

People's was nonprofit. That alone provided an additional $23,000 a year that the doctors could put in their pockets."

While it was clear that the clinic was doing important work in the community, Dick was concerned that people in Austin—those who were in a position to help—didn't know about the clinic or its work. "So I set out to increase public awareness of People's Community Clinic," he says. "Individuals who are well-known in the community needed to be involved."

To that end, Rathgeber enlisted the aid of a tennis buddy, Marvin Henderson, who was an oil and gas distributor. "I happened to know that Marvin was making some money right then, and he was also a very generous person," Rathgeber explains. "When I told him about People's Clinic, Marvin agreed to sponsor a series of four or five luncheons at the Headliners Club, each with a guest list of about seventy-five prominent people and potential donors in the community.

"With Marvin picking up the tab for the luncheons, I next needed a well-known and highly respected person or couple to serve as named host of these get-togethers," says Rathgeber. "I've always held that, when you're trying to raise money, it's important to have someone that people know and trust out front."

For this, he approached Walt Rostow, another of his tennis buddies. Rostow was the highly regarded American economist and political theorist who had served as special assistant for national security affairs to President Lyndon Baines Johnson. Along with his wife, Elspeth, Rostow was teaching at the Lyndon B. Johnson School of Public Affairs at the University of Texas. "Obviously the Rostows were widely connected to people of means in Austin," Dick concludes. "They were ideal to serve as named hosts of the luncheons for People's."

Another of Rathgeber's early enlistees was Dr. Robert Bernstein, former head of Walter Reed Hospital, who was now in Austin as the Texas commissioner of health. Former Texas lieutenant governor Ben Barnes helped Dick recruit Bernstein, who in turn lent his name and expertise to Dick's efforts in behalf of the People's Clinic.

With that, the fund drive was launched.

"Those luncheons were very effective," Rathgeber recalls. "We put on a regular dog-and-pony show. Roseanna and the clinic people stood up and told stories about what they were doing. It was during those luncheons that I learned it's easier to ask for $100,000 than for $1,000."

Asked what he means, Dick explains, "Well, if you ask someone for $1,000 and that person has limited means, the gift is a large percentage of the family income. It's going to be hard for him or her to give that $1,000. On the other hand, if you ask people with deep pockets for $1,000, they might wonder why you don't have enough faith in the organization to ask for a more substantial gift. The basic fact is, people of great wealth are likely to be giving generous gifts to *some* organization each year. It's up to the philanthropist to persuade them to give to a particular deserving group."

After those fund-raising luncheons, the people at People's Clinic realized that the building was only half as big as it needed to be. However, complicating any renovation was a storm sewer that cut right across the area where the addition needed to go. "Now, I knew something about storm sewers," says Dick, "so I got that moved and the easement changed."

Over the years Dick had approached the Austin Junior

League about supporting the clinic. The first two times, he was turned down, but in 1993 he received a call from a Junior League member who had been charged with finding a worthy cause to commemorate the League's sixtieth anniversary in Austin. "Right away, I had representatives from the Junior League meet me at the clinic. I walked them through the building, showed them the operation, and then took them to lunch at the Headliners. After a good lunch and some small talk, I asked them for $100,000."

"Actually," said one, "we wanted to do more. We wanted to give $250,000."

"In that case," Dick replied, "we'll call the annex the Junior League Annex."

In response to the burgeoning population that the clinic was serving, the size of the building was expanded from 8,000 to 16,000 square feet. A local architect, Jim Polkinghorn, donated his services, and today the building is beautifully decorated and warm.

"When you walk in," Dick says, "the atmosphere is friendly, and in no fashion does it feel impoverished. Thanks to the Austin Junior League, the new wing is tasteful and inviting. The clinic itself continues to be immensely efficient as it serves the working poor. It even added an on-site pharmacy, because many patients simply don't have the money to have prescriptions filled. So the People's Clinic Pharmacy offers prescriptions for about half the usual price."

When he describes a high return on philanthropic investment, Dick often cites his experience with the People's Clinic. "In fact, I consider this my best charitable effort," he says. "I've learned that the clinic is going to lose its present facility when I-35 is widened—so I'm saving them a site, just under four acres, at Rathgeber Village."

# Meals on Wheels

Meals on Wheels, operating in cities throughout the country, provides meals and companionship to people who are elderly, ill, or shut in. Rathgeber says, "The meals are only part of the service Meals on Wheels offers. This organization enables older people to stay in their homes, because volunteers deliver meals every day and check on the participants each time they deliver the food. The volunteers who deliver the meals often develop a bond with their clients, and they stop and visit. In addition, Meals on Wheels has a grocery-shopping service and a taxi service that takes elderly and infirm people to the doctor and other appointments."

According to Rathgeber, this is another organization that delivers terrific ROI. "In 2001, when the local Meals on Wheels decided to relocate because of space limitations, they asked me to help with their capital campaign," he says. "They approached me because, when they first came to town, my company had donated some demolition work for them. We hadn't been involved with them since then.

"Anyway, they needed to expand, and to do so they needed to move. Knowing that the first rule of fund-raising is that you have to give before you can ask others to give, Sara and I pledged $250,000 to their capital campaign.

"We had known Joe and Cherry Gray through our association at the Westwood Country Club and also through tennis. Joe played tournaments and was state-ranked. He had done very well in the insurance business, so I approached him for help. He and Cherry generously agreed to give $500,000, and in exchange the new facility was named for them. Meals on Wheels has been so successful here that already—in only seven years—it's needing to double its size again. They have a wonderful collaboration with the Capital

Area Food Bank to provide nutritious meals at a very reasonable rate, which enables them to expand their services to meet the local need. Sara and I made several contacts for that capital campaign, and in the end it was a successful campaign. Thousands of area residents have benefited."

Today Meals on Wheels is located east of I-35 on land that the organization owns—and it has enough land to expand as the need arises.

## The Settlement Club's Annual Garage Sale

Dick often reiterates his conviction that it's not always the amount of the monetary gift, in dollars and cents, that counts. Sometimes a smaller gift will reap amazing rewards. To him it's less a matter of giving much than it is of giving smart. To illustrate the point, he tells a story about a garage sale.

"The Settlement Home is a residential treatment center for abused girls in Austin. Every year the Settlement Club, which sponsors the home, has a giant garage sale to raise money in support of the home. Sara is a former president of the club, and she remains an active worker and supporter of the garage sale.

"Members and volunteers collect merchandise all year long, and store it in a warehouse until time for the big sale. Then my company routinely furnishes a majority of the trucks and the manpower to move the goods.

"The Saturday before the garage sale is move-in day, and I work harder that day than I do any day of the year, because I supervise the loading of the trucks. Why do I do that?" He grins. "Because Sara is committed to this organization and I want to keep sleeping in the big bed.

"Anyway, things progressed smoothly for years, as the

garage sale gained notice and kept growing. Then the ladies of the Settlement Club hit a snag. You see, for many years, the Settlement Club garage sale was held at the old city coliseum, and it did very well there. However, when that structure was torn down, the sale had to move to the Palmer Events Center, on Barton Springs Road. The city had an adjacent parking garage, and charged every car $7 to park during the garage sale. In addition, the Settlement Club ladies charged admission of $3 per person, as they always had. That meant people had to pay $10 or more just to attend.

"That first year the sale was held at the Palmer Center, it absolutely bombed! Attendance was off by forty percent, and at the end of the weekend they had truckload upon truckload of goods, clothes, and merchandise left unsold. Needless to say, they took in $150,000 less than they had the previous year.

"Discouraged, the ladies began to wonder whether the garage sale was effective as a money-raiser. They worried that its time was past.

"However, I thought I saw what the problem was: the ladies didn't understand poor people. I believed the garage sale, primarily, should be a means of transferring the good merchandise of West Austin to East Austin with dignity. To that end, I made a deal with the city to buy out the parking for the entire weekend for $7,000. What this meant was that the gate stayed up constantly, which in turn allowed traffic to move three to four times faster than when people had to stop and pay for parking.

"In addition, I told the Settlement Club that they absolutely *must not* charge admission on Saturday and Sunday, when the poor people would be shopping. This idea met with a great deal of opposition. 'But, Dick,' the ladies said, 'we've always done it this way.'

"I insisted, though, and in addition I persuaded one of my builder friends to run Spanish-language ads on the number one Spanish-language radio station in Austin, announcing that the garage sale would feature free parking and free admission. I told the ladies that I wanted this place to look like 'the front of the Alamo.'

"Well, that Saturday the sale grew from the 1,900 admissions of the previous year to 5,980. Sales increased by $150,000. And at the end of the sale, they had only half of one paper sack of unmatched socks left over. Every year since then, sales have set new records. I continue to pay for the parking—and these days nobody questions the viability of a garage sale.

"I figure that was not a bad way to invest $7,000."

## Giving Matching Funds

The Rathgebers are big supporters of the Assistance League of Austin. "This fine organization's chief source of fund-raising is a thrift store on Burnet Road," Dick says. "Its primary concern is providing school clothes for needy children. To that end they run a program called Operation School Bell, whereby they give each child who qualifies five complete school outfits. This has been a very successful program for them, and it's heartily endorsed by the Austin Independent School District. Within the last five years, they bought their own building and gained tremendous visibility. This was a really good move for them. They bought the building and did extensive fund-raising. Eventually, they got the balance owed on the building down to about $1.2 million.

"The fund drive sort of stalled at that point and that's

when our friend Stephanie Whitehurst contacted us for help. Sara and I thought the Assistance League was a very worthwhile cause, so we committed $120,000, payable at ten percent of what they collected each year. I had watched Michael and Susan Dell make contributions this way, and I saw that such gifts became a motivation for other donors. The first year, they collected $400,000, which we then matched with our gift of $40,000. This system is working quite well for the Assistance League."

SARA AND DICK ARE MEMBERS of St. Martin's Lutheran church on 15th Street in Austin. "About four years ago, the church did extensive renovations, which were sorely needed," Dick says, "because nothing had been done to the building since it was new in 1960. The 150th anniversary of the church is approaching, and some members decided it would be nice to be out of debt. The church still owes $1.6 million on a $4 million-plus project. Sara and I agreed to match twenty percent of what they raised in cash each year. The offer gave the fund drive new impetus, and the campaign is currently under way. I have no doubt that if St. Martin's gets enough people involved, it will be able to retire the debt. Offering matching funds is a means of encouraging others to participate, and at the same time it limits the amount that we are obligated to give. It's a system that works."

## DICK'S RULES FOR HOW TO APPROACH A PHILANTHROPIST

- My process is usually to request that a petitioner put the proposal in writing. Sometimes, though, I just talk to the person, and I say, 'Okay, first of all, what is your mission?' If a person can't give a passionate, knowledgeable account of what the organization is doing, I don't want to support it.

- Secondly, what's your budget, and did you meet it? Tell me about your administrative costs. You learn quickly whether this is a legitimate operation or just a salary source for the executive director, and believe me, there are a lot of those out there.

- These questions all boil down to one, which is how many people do you help, and at what cost? If my identity is that of a problem solver, then that's how I should approach these projects. What's the problem, and will my money or influence help solve it?

- How do I dispatch unworthy petitioners? I say, 'That's not a project that meets my guidelines.' It's strictly subjective.

- I've been wrong, though. There are some organizations that I didn't help initially, but later came back and helped.

# Do Something: Make Soup

On a wintry day in 2008, Rathgeber was shut in at his house. Roads in Austin were icy and closed, so he couldn't get out. Anyone who knows Dick knows he's a man of action. He moves fast, thinks fast, and makes connections, while slower, more deliberate colleagues are still considering the pros and cons of an idea. Rathgeber is not a man who enjoys being hobbled—by weather or any other obstacle. He wants to be *doing* something.

On this particular day, Dick made a few calls and eventually realized that the whole town was shut down. So? He went to the kitchen and rustled about for soup ingredients. "I have a bunch of elderly friends," says Rathgeber, himself seventy-five. "Some of them don't feel like cooking, so I often make soup to take around to them. It's a little thing, really, and it's something that anybody can do."

Dick has no shortage of ideas for how to help selected causes, large and small. He holds the view that people should believe strongly in a cause before they can help. "I always check an organization out before I throw my support behind it."

## Colleen Hagman

One person who came to Dick for advice about how to help an organization dear to her heart was Colleen Hagman, an Austin wife and mother. Colleen is married to Buddy Hagman, a longtime friend and business associate of Dick's, and she was recently charged with raising money for her favorite charity, the Rawson-Saunders School for Dyslexics.

"Buddy first knew Dick through banking," Colleen says, "and they became friends. My husband has a lot of respect for Dick, so when I was asked to head up the annual fund-raiser, he sent me to Dick for guidance."

The Hagmans have a personal interest in dyslexia. Colleen has it, for one thing, and by the time her children reached school age, she realized there were challenges ahead.

"In addition, I'm bipolar," Mrs. Hagman explains, "and one day when my daughter, Meagan, was in elementary school, another mother and I were comparing notes. I'd been asking questions about Meagan ever since she was in kindergarten. Even that early, she understood that she learned differently, and so we kept searching for the right place for her. She'd been to three schools, and nothing was working. Eventually, she asked me if she could be home schooled. I just wanted to find a place where she could learn."

Meagan was found to be dyslexic. Before much longer, her little brother, Drake, was similarly diagnosed. Mrs. Hagman recalls, "With two dyslexic children, I was overjoyed when I heard about Rawson-Saunders, a school custommade for Meagan and Drake. What a relief!"

Rawson-Saunders includes grades one through eight, but it can accommodate only about a hundred students. The goal of the school is to transition students to more traditional schools within two or three years. "With such a small enrollment," says Mrs. Hagman, "funds are always tight. Tuition is $16,000 per year per student, but that doesn't cover all the operating expenses, salaries, and so forth. Studies show that some thirty-five percent of identified learning-disabled students are dyslexic, and I wanted word of this great school to get out into the community. I wanted people to be aware that these kids, who too often fall through the cracks, can be helped."

Mrs. Hagman learned that the year before Meagan enrolled, the school almost had to close its doors because operating expenses were so high. "I can't imagine where Meagan would be today if Rawson-Saunders had closed. I knew I had to help. I found out the school had a gala every year to raise money," she explains, "and that year I was asked to chair the fund-raiser, which was set for April. I decided I really wanted to try something different this time, but what? That's when I went to Dick."

Colleen was nervous as she rang the doorbell at the Rathgebers' town home. "I knew they gave to a lot of important causes," she says, "but I wasn't there to ask for money. I wanted advice. I'd never done anything like this before."

She sat down with Dick, who immediately cut to the chase. "He said, 'Just tell me what you want to accomplish,' and I told him I wanted to reach out to the community. I told him there was such a crying need for this school, and I wanted to make sure people knew it was here.

"He heard me out, and then he said, 'If you want to make a lot of money and also get into the community, I think you should have a golf tournament.'"

Colleen goes on, a note of lingering amazement in her

voice. "A golf tournament? That would never have occurred to me. Dick said, 'You can have the whole event at Avery Ranch. Call the golf pro out there and use my name. You'll need to round up thirty-six teams. And after the tournament, you should have a dinner with a live auction. I'll help with the auction.'"

Rathgeber's enthusiasm is contagious, so the minute she left his house, Colleen called Brent, the golf pro at Avery Ranch, a residential neighborhood that Dick had developed a few years earlier. "A few days later, I went to talk to Brent," says Colleen. "I was so excited to be helping the school, and even more encouraged when I learned that Brent knew about dyslexia. I didn't have to explain a thing."

By now, in addition to her desire to help the school, Colleen found that she didn't want to disappoint Dick. She wanted to rise to his expectations. She says, "At the end of the evening, Dick and I were on the phone waiting to hear what we had raised. Even though this was the first time I ever fund-raised, I helped raise more than $85,000. I was overwhelmed. I had made a difference to a cause that was important to me. I'm not exaggerating when I say that that experience changed my life, and when the school asked me to commit for one more year, I did so readily."

Asked to elaborate, Mrs. Hagman replies, "Well, first of all, I didn't think I could do this. Dick taught me not to give a hoot what people think. He said if I believe in something enough, my passion will ignite passion in other people. He told me, 'You definitely have the passion for this. You can do it.' He believed in me before he even knew who I was, and certainly before I believed in myself. Dick understood there were two reasons I was up to the job. First of all, he understood the challenge of dyslexia, in part because he has a dyslexic grandson. And he saw the depth of my concern for the cause. He told me that if I cared that much, I just had to do what I could to help. He also taught me that when I'm raising money for a good cause, I'm giving others an opportunity to invest, as well as an opportunity to be significant."

## Kevin Robinson

In 1990, Kevin Robinson met Dick Rathgeber at the Headliners Club, where Dick is a regular. As already noted, the Headliners is the site of many of his meetings and deal-making lunches. In 1990, he began noticing a young African American man who worked there, Kevin Robinson.

"At the time, I was just a busboy," Robinson recalls, "but for some reason Mr. Rathgeber took a liking to me. One day he asked me what school I went to. I told him I had graduated from high school and that I'd gone to Blinn College in Bryan/College Station. Later I had taken classes at Austin Community College, but by the time I met Mr. Rathgeber, I had a little girl. I needed to work to support her. 'I guess I won't have any more chances to go to school,' I told him.

"Mr. Rathgeber started nagging me about that. Every time I saw him, he told me again that I should be back in school. I explained that it had been a while since I was in school, and I wasn't even sure how many hours I had, or how to get my transcripts. Then one day he said, 'Look, Kevin, if I get your transcript, will you go back to school?' I said yes, but it had been years since I'd been in school. I doubted he could round up my transcripts. He did, though, and then I had to make good on my part of the deal.

"True to my word, I started taking information technology classes at Austin Community College. These were the early days of IT, and I found myself rolling in on the boom. Before long I started changing some things at work. I put everybody's hours on spreadsheets, for example, making it possible for management to monitor workers' hours. Always before, those records had been written out by hand. People just came in when they came in, and they didn't leave until the work was done. By standardizing these records, we were able to curb overtime at the club, and thereby curb labor costs.

"Soon I was working my way up through the ranks. Even so, Mr. R. kept riding me about college. Eventually he made me a deal. He told me that if I would finish a managerial course offered through extended learning at the University of Texas, he'd ease up on me about school. So I did that. I completed seven courses, and I earned that coveted managerial certificate.

"Mr. Rathgeber was so happy for me. He wanted to throw a party just for me at the Headliners Club. I told him I didn't need a party, but he insisted. 'What would you like?' he asked me.

"'Let me think about it,' I said.

"The next day I called him and I said that instead of his doing a party for me, I wanted to do something for my kids. 'I'll tell them that you stayed on me to get an education, and I'm going to stay on them,' I told him."

Kevin was coaching a select basketball team called the Rising Stars. "The team was made up of boys age thirteen and under. I was a volunteer coach for them, and I decided to have a party with them at Dick's house. That evening, each kid got a sweat suit with his name monogrammed on it. These kids were all in school, but they needed inspiration to stay there. They were all from different backgrounds. Some had single parents, some lived with their grandparents, some knew their father and others didn't.

"In other words, they were growing up in the same situation that I grew up in. When I was growing up, my real father was never around. My stepfather was in the house, but I resented him until I got older and started to understand the value he brought to my life by being with my mom and helping us out financially. Boys need to learn early in life that if there's a man in your house, he deserves respect. Many of these boys didn't have a father figure.

"What I learned from Dick Rathgeber is to take good fortune and pass it on."

Kevin had a particular plan for how he could pass his own good fortune on. His best friend, Ray Jackson, had been one of the Fab Five in Michigan. "This was considered the top college recruiting class of all time," explains Kevin. "They took five fabulous high school players from all over the country and got them to be the freshman class at the University of Michigan. Ray was one of those. His dad was the coach at LBJ High School here in Austin, and Ray and I grew up as high school teammates and best friends. Now he helps run my academic and athletic program, which is called Rise Up, Inc. This is my own private boys and girls program. It's actually a life program. I'll bet I get two calls a day from parents letting me know when a kid has a basketball game. Mr. Rathgeber helps fund us. For example, he made it possible for the boys to fly to Indiana the last two years, to compete in the national USSSA basketball championships. When we go places like that, it's the first time some of the boys have ever been away from home, first time out of the city."

Rathgeber was not content with nudging Kevin to get

ahead at work. After a time, he suggested that Kevin be named to the board of the Salvation Army. "My role there is to show the Salvation Army how to really help the kids," Kevin says. "I urge them not to give kids things, but to make the youngsters feel as though they've earned it. If you give a child a handout, he'll always want the handout. The trick is to make children feel empowered."

Today, Kevin Robinson is assistant manager of the Headliners Club, where he continues to take great pride in his work.

## Ann Phipps

Ann Phipps is a young Austin matron who recently went to Dick for philanthropic advice. "My family has a foundation," Ann explains. "It's named for my father, Charles H. Phipps, who worked as an engineering manager throughout his career and then, around 1988, retired and picked up a second career in venture capital. He did very well.

"Dad had grown up in a family that believed giving was important. His was a family of quiet givers. With the benefit of these resources from venture capital, Dad found himself with a lot of money, so he and my mother were able to think about giving in larger ways. They established this foundation so that the four of us—my parents, my brother, and I—could help worthy causes."

Ann's parents, now in their eighties, took care of the legal part of forming the foundation. "It's commonly done and not actually that complicated," she says. "In fact, you don't have to have all that much money. You can start a foundation with as little as $100,000. The only thing is, you have to give away a certain percentage of the money every year. Grants won't be large, but a person can do a lot with, say, a $5,000 grant."

The Phipps Foundation gives generously to programs in Dallas, including the Sisters of Charity, the group founded by Mother Teresa. "The Sisters never ask for anything," Phipps points out, "and they help the poorest of the poor."

It was arranged that Ann would be responsible for a portion of the foundation's resources, and that she would be able to choose how that portion was spent. Since she lives in Austin, she wanted to use the money in her hometown. But where?

"I knew Dick and Sara Rathgeber through my mother-in-law, who was in the Settlement Club with Sara," Ann says. "Also, I had attended a dinner and auction that Meals on Wheels held to celebrate Dick a few years earlier. The auction was by far the biggest fundraiser the group had ever had. It was so funny to watch Dick that evening, as he went around the room during the auction, pointing at people and saying, 'It's your turn to bid.' I knew then that he would be a great person to ask for guidance as I learned what it means to give to charity."

Phipps says that her family's foundation focuses on education, the mentally retarded, and what they call "people on the margins."

"I've advocated for repeating grants to programs that especially interest me, such as Meals on Wheels. Another is the Saint Louise House, which offers lodging to homeless women with children, allowing qualified women to live for six to eighteen months without expense, and also to receive support services," she says.

She is always on the lookout for good causes, and sometimes they come from unexpected sources. "A year or so ago, I read an article in the *Wall Street Journal* about a backpack program that philanthropists had started in various cities. As I read, I learned about a problem I'd never considered, one that surfaced when a school nurse noticed that children were coming to school on Mondays too hungry to sit up. It soon came to light that these children hadn't eaten at all over the weekend, and when people recognized the problem, efforts were made to figure out how to provide weekend food for these children. Their parents were overwhelmed, often working two shifts, and the children simply couldn't depend on the adults in their lives to take care of them. That's when someone came up with the backpack program."

Targeting children from kindergarten through elementary school, the backpack program provides kid-friendly but nutritious foods packed in a backpack and sent home with the children over weekends. "I cried reading how these children were being helped," Phipps recalls, "and I didn't think anybody was doing this in Austin. I knew Dick was connected to a number of food-based charities, so I called him and told him I wanted to do a similar program here. 'We need to find out if anybody's doing it,' I told him. 'How do we do that?'

"He connected me to Judy Carter at the Capital Area Food Bank. This was in 2006. When I called Judy, she said, 'It's great that you called, because these programs are expanding all over the country, and many are connected to food banks.' She added that her organization had tried a pilot program at a school in a low-income area of East Austin the previous summer, and that it had been a big success. In fact, they'd been trying to figure out how to ramp it up. Of course, the food bank would be a logical partner, because it had access to food items that such a program would require—such as fruit and cereal."

Very soon, the Capital Area Food Bank sent Phipps a proposal noting that to qualify for the pack program a child has to qualify for government aid through the free-lunch program. The school they'd served in the pilot program seemed a good place to start, because literally every kid in the school qualified, which meant that nobody would be stigmatized.

"Once we were established, I went over to see how the program was working. What I saw was that everybody lines up after lunch on Fridays, gets his or her groceries, and puts them in his backpack. All the kids seemed so happy, and the principal told me that school attendance has increased on Fridays, because children have to come to school in order to get their groceries."

Ann and her family have left it to the food bank to decide how to distribute their grant, and she adds, "We haven't promised anything for after three years. We want the program to find other funding to keep itself going. We think of our gift as seed money."

Asked about his part in the process, Dick Rathgeber says, "All I did was to connect Ann with the right people, and remind her that the food bank had the necessary infrastructure already in place. Her timing was propitious, because the food bank had already carried out a pilot program, and they were ready to move forward."

# If You Crash,
# Pick Yourself Up

People who don't know Dick and Sara except from what they read in the newspaper or hear from various nonprofits can be forgiven for assuming that the Rathgebers have always lived a charmed life. Today, all evidence points to their steadily rising star in the Austin business and philanthropic worlds.

However, this Horatio Alger version of their life leaves out an important chapter, one that Dick finds difficult to talk about even now, almost twenty years later.

In the late 1980s and early 1990s, Austin experienced a real estate crash. The city had overbuilt, nobody was buying, and therefore property values had fallen through the cellar. Thousands of people—builders, developers, Realtors, homeowners, and others only remotely connected to real estate—found themselves caught in the downward spiral. Banks tightened their lending requirements, but they were pulled into the economic undertow as well. Some banks merged and others shut down. Individuals, corporations, and individual investors declared bankruptcy.

Dick Rathgeber was pulled under as well. On July 14, 1990, the *Austin American-Statesman* ran the following front-page story.

## CITY PHILANTHROPIST, INVESTOR RATHGEBER FILES BANKRUPTCY
by Kim Tyson,
*Austin American-Statesman*

Dick Rathgeber, a local philanthropist who donated $2 million in downtown land to the Salvation Army, has filed for liquidation of his assets under federal bankruptcy laws.

Rathgeber, a millionaire real estate investor during Austin's boom, was named "1985 Austinite of the Year" by the Austin Chamber of Commerce after his donation solved a major problem for the Salvation Army.

At the time, the Salvation Army had been searching fruitlessly in several neighborhoods, all of which opposed a center for the homeless. The city was concerned about giving money to buy the site because of legal issues over separation of church and state.

But longtime Salvation Army supporter Rathgeber resolved the dilemma by trading land he owned to come up with the East Eighth Street site that he donated.

Rathgeber, 57, said Friday that his financial problems stem from the fallout in the Austin real estate and financial industries. He filed late Thursday for Chapter 7 liquidation of Southwest Rathgeber Co., a real estate investment and con-

(Continued on next page)

tracting company, and personal bankruptcy for himself and his wife, Sara.

In his personal bankruptcy, he said, he and his wife have between 50 and 99 creditors who together are owed more than $1 million. They also list assets of more than $1 million. For Southwest Rathgeber Co., he estimates it has 16 to 49 creditors, assets of less than $50,000 and liabilities of more than $1 million. Specific lists of creditors, assets, and liabilities will be filed at a later date.

"I basically got caught in the same avalanche that the banks and S&Ls did," Rathgeber said. He said nearly all his debts are to lenders on real estate projects.

"There are no subcontractors and no material accounts or small business people or anything like that."

He said he had sold most of his real estate holdings at one time. But many buyers later defaulted on their purchases, and by then the real estate market had collapsed.

His University Business Park in South Austin was hurt during the boom, when the city issued a moratorium on sewer taps after he had contracts on all the lots in the development. He owned 320 acres on Comanche Trail that were later found to be the habitat of the endangered black-capped vireo. He said he had a contract to sell more than a third of the Comanche Trail land for what he owed on the total tract when the project was stopped because of the bird.

Rathgeber said federal financial regulators this spring forced him to file for bankruptcy. He said new rules obstructed the agreements he had pursued with banks.

"I've been pushing this boulder up the hill the whole time and then the Resolution Trust Corp. comes along and says, 'Don't worry about that boulder because we've got sev-

(Continued on next page)

eral more dump trucks full of boulders coming.' So in a way it was kind of a relief," he said.

Rathgeber said most of his property was repossessed by lenders this spring, including a 3,000-acre ranch on FM 1431 on Lake Travis that he said he once had contracts on for $34 million.

"The only thing I know to do is to dig myself out of the avalanche, dust myself off and start all over again," he said.

"I'm really extremely fortunate, just really blessed," said Rathgeber, the son of a Lutheran minister. His home, which is protected under bankruptcy laws, was paid off eight years ago, he said. He plans to work for a contracting firm owned by his son and two daughters, Southwest Constructors, which is not involved in the bankruptcies.

"You know there is a saying that the most terrible truth is never worse than uncertainty," he said of his situation. "I don't feel bad about it at all because it's just one of those things that happened. What have there been, over 20,000 [bankruptcy] filings? There are some people who ought to file and get on with their lives, particularly attorneys.

"This has been an opportunity to show my faith in God and the future," Rathgeber said. "I could go around with my tail in the dirt or I could dig out and dust myself off and get on down the road."

Rathgeber said he can continue to have good feelings about his donations to the Salvation Army and other charities, including the Settlement Home, Girl Scouts and Junior Helping Hand Home. He also was a major contributor to the construction of League Houses around the state that provide housing near hospitals for the families of critically ill patients.

(Continued on next page)

This spring, Lutheran Social Services of Texas honored him with a dinner at the Doubletree Hotel.

Rathgeber said one former Methodist minister once told him, "The only thing you can't lose is the thing you've given away."

AT THE TIME OF HIS FINANCIAL COLLAPSE, Dick had a tennis buddy named Guy Bodine. "Guy was the number two man at First Republic Bank, which was a merger between Republic Bank and InterFirst," Dick says. "Previously, it had been Austin National Bank. I had been on the board of the bank, but I'd known Guy for a long time before that. He was both my banker and a friend, so he had firsthand knowledge of my situation. I filed for bankruptcy during an era of bank mega-mergers. The FDIC was getting rid of low-performing banks, so it wasn't an easy time for bankers either."

Bodine agrees. "Most of Austin was involved in the real estate business in one way or another. There were far more projects than the market could absorb. The reason the prices dropped so dramatically was that there were no buyers. If you build five spec houses and there's no one to buy them, that property suddenly has a much lower value. There were countless projects all over the city: too many projects, too few buyers. Of course, I was a part of all that myself. In fact, my situation was worse than most: I was the lender.

"In good times, people comport themselves well, but it's in hard times that you see their true character. When times were good, Dick was riding high. As you must know, he enjoys the limelight, so when the economy was booming, Dick was out in front, an extraordinarily generous man. But what I saw in the bad times, particularly in the early 1990s, was that Dick continued to use whatever resources he had, which by then were diminished, to do good in the community. The scale of his giving was not as large, but he never lost that sense of responsibility to the community. You see, there was a natural tendency during those years to hide out, to run away, but I never saw Dick do that. Instead, he went directly to the newspaper and told them what was going on."

At one point—when he thought things couldn't get worse—Dick received the alarming news that his children might be held liable for some of his debt. "I became aware of the law of joint and several liability, which holds that a person who has, say, a five percent interest in a company can be held liable for a hundred percent of its debt. What that meant to me was that my children could be involved in my bankruptcy. I could never allow this. So I went to the bank and said, 'I'm here to negotiate a hostage release.'

"Lew Little, a vice president of the bank, said, 'That's too harsh a term.'

"'You wouldn't think so if it were your kids who were involved,' I told him. 'Now here's the deal. In combing through my records, I found $700,000 that's unencumbered. You let my kids off the hook and you can have this $700,000, which is all I've got. If you don't like that, you can pick cow patties with the chickens.'"

Dick then proceeded to remind his colleagues that, in a barnyard, the chickens all cluster around fresh cow patties in order to pick out whatever seeds and grain have made their way through.

"It's up to you," he finished.

The bankers agreed to his terms. Later, of course, the bank itself went broke.

FOR THIRTY-SEVEN YEARS, until she died in December 2007, Lou Ann Montey was the Rathgebers' CPA. In a conversation before her death, she recalled Dick's anguish during those days when his business was crumbling. "It was so sad. He had all these partnerships, all these notes on lands, etc., and when the bottom fell out on the real estate business, the banks came in and revalued the real estate collateral. The difference between the value of the land and what he owed on it could amount to millions of dollars. He had no choice but to file bankruptcy.

"He called me the night before the story of his crash was going to hit the papers, and he was so down. Everybody was filing bankruptcy, yet it's a very personal thing. I think Dick finally satisfied himself, through many conferences and meetings, that he had no other choice. Still, he was so disheartened. I told him, 'Listen, you may be down now, but in five years, you're going to be riding high. You're going to call me crying about how much tax you owe.' And I was right.

"When he did file Chapter 7, though, I was amazed. The matter was handled very nicely. There weren't a bunch of nasty comments in the press. People took into consideration the type of man he is. He's honorable, a straight shooter. He's going to tell it like it is, whether you like it or not.

"I hate to see people who are flippant about filing bankruptcy. Bankruptcy is a serious business."

Adds Guy Bodine, "That was a painful time for everybody. Young people who haven't been through this kind of thing look at somebody like Dick and they tend to think that person has never had hard times. But a great entrepreneur in Dallas once told me he talks more about what didn't work in his career than what did. That's where, he said, he learned the most."

Asked what he thinks Rathgeber learned from his bankruptcy, Guy replies, "A level of humility. Courage. Just think what it took to go to the newspaper, how courageous that was. And when you confront those dark days, it enhanced Dick's faith—in himself, in the future. To go from being a person who carried such a positive profile, who had done so well, who'd built his resources up from nothing—to go from that to bankruptcy was humbling. I watched plenty of others who weren't so resilient."

Bodine points to Dick's integrity under stress. "Dick never lost sight of his obligation to nonprofits. In a way, it's the economic nature of this community that has created Dick. He has given, consistently and generously, over a long period of time. And it's not just the money. I suspect that there are many people out there whom he has helped who will never know about it.

"I think his bankruptcy, oddly enough, was his finest hour."

AFTER THE ARTICLE APPEARED in the newspaper, the Rathgebers received hundreds of letters, cards, and phone calls from friends, politicians, nonprofits, Salvation Army officers, and many ordinary people whom they had helped. Messages were uniformly encouraging, and all pointed to the writers' confidence that Dick would soon be back on his feet. One letter in particular touched Dick. It was from a former business partner, a man who had fronted the money for one of Dick's development projects. The businessman wrote, "Let me reiterate what I have told numerous people: you were a perfect partner to me. I would be more than delighted for you to be my partner again."

Another friend paraphrased a Hemingway line from *A Farewell to Arms*, saying, "The world breaks everyone, but some become strong at the broken place. I know this will be your way."

Letter after letter arrived at the Rathgeber house, each offering solace, encouragement, and admiration. Armed with determination and a wide circle of friends and supporters, Dick and Sara, as promised, "picked themselves up, dusted themselves off, and started all over again."

# Dealing with Crooks

"When it comes to dealing with crooks, I can give you lots of examples. But I've decided that I don't want to go through life mistrusting everybody. I want to trust, but not naively. I figure I'll trust everybody until I find out something that merits my distrust.

"It happens to everybody in business. Sooner or later you find yourself dealing with a person who is dishonest, who isn't guided by conscience, or a basic sense of right and wrong. When this happens, it has nothing to do with you and everything to do with them. You can't blame yourself. Just go on down the road. Don't try to get even. Just avoid them from then on. Crooks are crooks.

"Once I set a young man up in the appliance business and when I got ready to shut the business down, I found out the inventory was $180,000 short because, among other things, he had been trading appliances for elegant jewelry for his wife. When I confronted him, he admitted it. He told me he'd been thinking about suicide, but I didn't want that blood on my hands. I just walked away. I go by the rule of what I have to gain and what I have to lose. In this case, filing charges would have gained me nothing, and it would have ruined that young family's life. So I decided not to prosecute, because the guy had a lovely wife and two small kids, and he wasn't going to be able to pay me anyway. So I just shut the business down and took my licks.

"But needless to say, he would not be getting any job recommendations from me."

"ANOTHER STORY INVOLVES St. Martin's Lutheran Church, downtown," Dick says. "The building was built in 1960, and nothing had been done to update it in the years between then and the year 2000. The carpets were worn, and the location of the organ had changed, so there was a tattered curtain at the front of the church where the organ was originally supposed to be positioned. By 2001, the church needed a shave and a haircut.

"This was a time of a real building boom in Austin, and therefore it was difficult to find a contractor who wanted to do the job. We took bids and awarded the contract to the low bidder. Very soon it became apparent that he was less than ethically stellar. We learned this when we became aware that he was not paying his subcontractors in a timely manner.

"When he finally finished the job, he owed a tremendous amount of money to the subcontractors. Most of the bills he was holding were more than ninety days old, so they would not have been covered by the mechanic's lien law."

According to the Department of Consumer Affairs, a mechanic's lien is a "hold" against property that, if unpaid, allows a foreclosure action, forcing the sale of your home.

It is recorded with the County Recorder's office by the un-paid contractor, subcontractor or supplier. Sometimes liens occur when the prime contractor has not paid subcontrac-tors or suppliers. Legally, the homeowner is ultimately re-sponsible for payment—even if they have already paid the prime contractor.

RATHGEBER GOES ON, "The mechanic's lien law stipulates that the subcontractor has to file a claim within ninety days of the last day he did any work. In other words, bills must be paid within ninety days of the time the work is done. Obviously, the church could be held liable if the contractor didn't pay his men. We were very concerned.

"When the time came to settle up, we asked the con-tractor for a list of everything and everybody he owed. Then we made out joint checks, with his name and that of the company owed the money on the same check. We scheduled a meeting with the church trustees, the business manager, and Sam Zumwalt, our pastor at the time. That contractor came into the meeting with a big stack of checks already made out, and he said, 'As soon as you pay me, I'll mail these checks.' We replied that it wasn't going to work quite that way. We had already heard from the sub-contractors that they hadn't been paid, so we gave him all the joint checks, plus checks for what we still owed him. The contractor became furious. He appealed to Pastor Sam, saying, 'That's not the way you would do business, is it?'

"Pastor Sam smiled and said, 'I just watch people's feet.' We knew that if we had not done it this way, the sub-contractors would not have been paid.

"A philosophy that has worked for me is, 'It's better that I have the money and you're mad, than that you have the money and I'm mad.' I knew that contractor was going to skip town and we'd never have heard from him again. But with these two-signature checks, if he tried to sign and deposit them, he would be committing bank fraud and the bank would have to cover the charges, because the signatures would be forged.

"I've had to take this action several times through the years. Say I have a painter who wants money for paints. I'll simply call the paint store and ask if they're being paid for supplies. Then I offer to make out a joint check. If the store says no, then I ask them to send me a letter to that effect. This works for people having work done on their houses or any other project. I make sure the supplier is being paid. It's easy enough to pick up the phone and double-check.

"A person learns this the hard way. Once our company got hit for $50,000 because our contractor sent us a check on about the eighty-seventh day, and by the time we found out the check was hot, the statute of limitations had expired. We had to eat that cost, and that happened right as we were coming back from bankruptcy.

"Today, the crimes have become ever more sophisticated. An apartment manager that I trusted figured out a way to wire-transfer money out of my account in one bank to an account that he opened in my name—without my knowledge—in another bank. As a result, the two banks are arguing about who dropped the ball, and meanwhile I'm out $52,000. I wouldn't have known anything about it except that Sara happened to notice it in looking over our books.

"Crooks are out there. My advice on how to deal with them: Don't."

# Giving Land: Rathgeber Village

It's notable how many overlapping projects and people Dick is involved with at any given time. Asked how he keeps it all straight, he says, "It's true I always have a lot of pots on the stove, but I only stir the ones that are boiling. It's mainly a matter of keeping things moving forward. When you're working on a charitable project, you don't have any competition, and that simplifies things somewhat. By contrast, if you're working on a for-profit deal, there's *always* competition."

Perhaps the most representative example of Rathgeber's multi-tiered interests is the emerging Rathgeber Village, a sprawling parcel of land that, within only a few years, will be home to the headquarters of several Austin nonprofits.

To start at the beginning: In the mid-1990s, the city of Austin decided to move its municipal airport to the former Bergstrom Air Force Base a few miles southeast of downtown. When the new Austin Bergstrom International Airport opened in 1999, the Robert Mueller Airport was left vacant. All runways were disabled, and this large plot of land east of Interstate 35 stood empty for months. It was clear to everyone that the area should be redeveloped, and city fathers, politicians, and developers all had ideas about how that should come about.

Rathgeber had ideas, too, and as plans evolved, he began what would become the most far-reaching of his contributions to the city.

As ways to use this large and strategically located plat of land were being mulled over, none of this was clear. "I put together a development team to bid on redeveloping the parcel," Dick explains. "I thought the plan the city had endorsed, and that they expected everyone to follow, would not work. In addition to the reasons I've already enumerated, it was clear that any site east of I-35 was considered a B location, at best, which meant that no financing would be available. Even if tenants wanted to locate there—which I doubted—they would have had enormous problems getting the necessary funding."

Despite his doubts about the plan, Rathgeber and his partners put an application together. "But we refused to submit a pro forma on the city's plan, because, as I've already said, we believed it would not work."

Rathgeber's competitor for the project was a San Francisco company, Catellus, which was then redeveloping the old San Francisco Railyard. Says Rathgeber, "When we watched the presentation Catellus put on for the city, my partners and I were blown away, and so was everybody else. It was altogether clear that Catellus was better qualified for the job than we were, and ultimately Catellus was selected to do the Mueller redevelopment."

All along, Sara Rathgeber had hoped her husband wouldn't be selected for the project. She could see how extensive it would be, and how much of a toll it would take on him. "I always joke that the reason I didn't get the job was that Sara was praying so hard that I wouldn't," Dick says with a wry grin.

If he was disappointed to be beaten out, Rathgeber didn't have time to notice, because immediately he was on to a new plan. "While I had been driving around looking at the airport land to get my proposal together," he says, "I noticed there was an eighteen-acre parcel immediately adjacent to the airport plat. It looked as though it was a part of the airport, but actually it wasn't."

Rathgeber saw a faded *For Sale* sign on the property, and, as he says, "I started chasing the deal." It took almost a year, but eventually he was able to buy that land for $1 million.

"I thought it would make an ideal venue for nonprofits," he says, "because it was close to the new redevelopment and it was close to downtown. I was convinced the redevelopment of the airport was going to change the character of the surrounding neighborhoods."

Dick could see that his newly acquired land was perfectly positioned to allow deserving nonprofits the room to spread out. "The most obvious prospect for the new location was the Austin Children's Shelter," he says. The shelter is a home that provides emergency housing and care to abandoned, abused, and neglected children. The shelter was housed in two single-family dwellings on one of the busiest thoroughfares in Austin, and it was terribly crowded. "The neighborhood absolutely refused to let the shelter expand," Rathgeber explains, "so it was stuck with a capacity of approximately thirty children. Sometimes that became a problem, particularly if they had teenagers of the opposite sex in residence. Eventually, the shelter had to take all the doors off the bedrooms, so nobody had privacy. It was far from an ideal situation.

"It became immediately apparent that expanding the children's shelter would be a project of great magnitude. It would require plenty of fund-raising, and help would be needed from a variety of sources. I had known Gary Farmer since the 1980s, and I've always had tremendous respect for him. He had recently raised $13 million for the Chamber of Commerce on an $11.5 million goal. I knew I wanted Farmer on my team. Together we organized a group to take on the fund-raising for the Austin Children's Shelter, and we called them 'Fighter Pilots.' Knowing that the kind of people we wanted would have a very short attention span and would not be content to sit in long meetings, we got Lee Walker, head of Capital Metro, as our honorary co-chairman. We also enlisted Mary Scott Nabors, a leading public relations professional; Richard Topfer from the Topfer Foundation; and Beth Stabile, who was on the shelter board and who had contacts in the high-tech industry. Ben Barnes's help was of great value as well, because he gave us introductions to people like Wayne Reaud, who had created the Beaumont Foundation of America. Wayne and his wife, Dana, subsequently contributed $1 million to build the administration building for the shelter. Other generous donors were Bill and Pat Munday, who originally gave $500,000 to build one of the cottages.

"A few weeks later, at a party at the Naborses' house, I saw the Mundays talking animatedly with my wife, Sara. Bill and Pat were asking why we needed a separate school building on the campus. Sara explained that the kids at the shelter were often so traumatized that they were set up for failure in a normal school setting, and that they just played hooky until it was time to go back to the shelter. As I walked by, Bill Munday remarked, 'Hey, Rathgeber, your wife is a heck of a lot better fund-raiser than you are.' I replied, 'Hey, I never said I was any good.' He said, 'That school is $900,000, isn't it?' and I said, 'No. It's a million.' To that he said, 'Well, send somebody by my office next week and I'll give them a check. I want to buy that school.'

"At the same party were Mrs. Martha Kutscher and her niece, Dr. Kathryn Kotrla, who had given seventy acres of land worth $700,000 to the children's shelter project, in exchange for naming rights to the infants and toddlers cottage. Also, Kim and Bob Wunsch donated funds for one of the cottages, as did the Topfer Foundation. In addition to serving as capital campaign chairman, Gary and Susan Farmer donated $500,000. We have had grants from numerous foundations, such as the Mabee, the Meadows, the Kresge, as well as the City of Austin, Travis County, and countless generous individual donors who have put us very close to our goal of $12.9 million."

As word of the Rathgebers' plans filtered out into the community, people began to realize that nonprofits would be locating on the land Dick had bought. The Rathgebers were soon contacted by other groups as well.

Rathgeber's original vision was to fill the land with facilities offering services to children. But then Family Eldercare approached him. At Family Eldercare, elders and adults with disabilities are supported in a community where they live with dignity and as much independence as possible. The organization provides essential services for these deserving people and those who care for them. "As I thought about it," says Rathgeber, "I realized the elderly are sometimes abused as much as, or more than, children are. Family Eldercare was crowded and in desperate need of a new location. That deserving nonprofit does important work and treats people with compassion. It gives hope to people who need hope. So I adjusted my plans to make a site available to them."

With that, Children's Village evolved into Rathgeber Village. "Next I decided to save a place for People's Community Clinic. I'd been involved with People's for a long time, and I knew the clinic would be losing its location when I-35 is widened in a few years. Its parking lot comes right up to the access road of the freeway, so obviously the land on which the clinic now sits will be condemned. I put aside a large site for People's, knowing that sometime in the future they will need it badly."

As Dick's plans grew, it became apparent that Rathgeber Village would have to be developed in at least two phases. Phase I would include these three: the Austin Children's Shelter, Family Eldercare, and the site for People's Community Clinic.

No sooner had these decisions been made than Dick started thinking about Phase II. The Mueller development plan included the Dell Children's Hospital and a planned community of more than two thousand single-family homes, so it was clear the community would need an elementary school. Says Rathgeber, "I'm in the process of joint-venturing approximately twenty-four acres with the Austin Independent School District so that AISD can build an elementary school there."

Also in the plan for Phase II of Rathgeber Village is a Kroc Center. The Ray and Joan Kroc Foundation, courtesy of the McDonald's restaurant fortune, helps cities throughout the country build community centers.

"The Kroc Foundation has given $1.625 billion to the Salvation Army nationally for use in building community centers throughout the United States," Dick explains. "The Salvation Army decides where these centers will be built. In every case in the southern territory, it's a two-to-one match. In other words, the Kroc funds two-thirds, and the community is supposed to raise the remaining one-third. However, the Salvation Army has a unique way of calculating the community's contribution. Gifts, wills, and bequests, as well as the sale of existing property can be counted toward a city's obligation. In Austin's case, the Salvation Army sold its old site to a local developer for condos, and that $4.5 million counts as part of Austin's one-third obligation. Sara and I donated the land, which is worth $3 or $4 million, and this also counts as part of Austin's obligation. When all the money comes in, Austin will need to raise only about $10 million. In total, we will raise $20 million and the Kroc Foundation will match it to the tune of $40 million."

The Rathgebers are giving the land for the Kroc Center to a donor designated trust under the Austin Community Foundation. "The ACF will sell that land to the Salvation Army," Dick explains, "which means they pay $3 million and they get $3 million back. In effect, they're getting a free site for the Kroc Center."

He goes on, "Each Kroc Center is unique to the city in which it is located. In our case, it was decided that we needed a top-notch, two-hundred-child day care center. So we are planning one in cooperation with the University of Texas. U.T. students will be able to do their lab work and practice teaching just as if they were on the main campus of U.T. In addition, we're going into a day care certification program with the U.T. Adult Education Department. In this program, students can do on-the-job training and become certified as day care center workers. This training is for working adults and returning students, as well as regular undergraduates. Anybody can go through the training."

In the end, if all goes as planned, the Ray and Joan Kroc Center will occupy about five acres. Dick also wants to include the Boys and Girls Clubs, so they have been granted two acres. The Boys and Girls Club and the Kroc Center will back up to a shared playground with the new elementary school.

Additionally, the Rathgebers pledged five acres and $2.5 million cash to the Austin Independent School District for a performing arts center.

As of this writing, the Austin Children's Shelter building project is well under way, and the Kroc Center is slated to open its doors in 2012. Phase II, Rathgeber hopes, will include an elementary school, the Kroc day care center and training program, the Boys and Girls Clubs, and a brand-new, state-of-the-art, 1,200-seat performing arts center for AISD. But that's another story. . . .

## Robert Mueller Airport Redevelopment Project

The master plan at the former Robert Mueller Airport provides for some 2,200 homes in a planned community that reflects the spirit of Austin. There will be four distinct neighborhoods in this urban development, each featuring places to shop, work, and play. Wide streets, playgrounds, and a nearby school will mean that Mueller residents can find whatever they need within walking distance. Bus stops on each corner will connect residents to downtown Austin and the rest of the city.

Inspired by the traditional Austin neighborhoods, the development will be diverse, offering houses with yards, row houses, and structures that feature shops below and living quarters above, as well as mixed-use apartments and townhouses. It's hoped that this variety of living spaces will attract people of varied lifestyles and incomes to a planned community in the heart of north central Austin.

# Navigating Through Bureaucracy

According to Rathgeber, philanthropy and bureaucracy often go hand in hand, and it's sometimes the case that the larger the gift a person is trying to give, the more necessary it becomes to plow through bureaucratic tangles.

"My first and most important piece of advice to an entrepreneur who finds himself dealing with a bureaucracy is to make connections with the right people," he says. "You simply have to reach the person in charge. It does no good to speak with those who are lower down on the ladder.

"One practical concern in making contact with an individual, especially if you're trying to make an appointment for lunch or a meeting," Rathgeber says, "is to find out who the person's gatekeeper is. Usually the secretary keeps the boss's schedule and makes his or her appointments. It's important that you create a positive impression with that person, so he or she will see you as someone the boss should pay attention to. You call the secretary and say, 'I need to talk to your boss.' Confide what it's about and ask, 'What can you do to help me?' Very often, she will check the calendar and say, 'Well, he has some time on such-and-such a day,' and she'll schedule you in. Other times, all you need to do is talk to the secretary on the phone. Say, 'Will you do me a favor? When your boss gets off the phone, will you please dial my number and tell him that I'm holding for him?' More often than not the secretary will do this, because you have empowered her.

"And here's another important tip: after your meeting, always call the gatekeeper back and say thanks for the help she gave you. In fact, saying thanks is important across the board. Once I called an editorial writer at the newspaper to thank her for an outstanding editorial, and she said, 'Oh, Mr. Rathgeber, in my entire journalistic career, this is the first time anybody has ever called to thank me.'"

Dick doesn't have a gatekeeper himself. He keeps his own schedule, lists himself and Sara in the phone book, and even declines caller ID. "I answer my own phone and make my own appointments," he says, "though many calls I receive wind up being NFL, meaning 'not for long.' The telephone is a fantastic tool for business, but it's important to learn how to terminate a conversation politely."

Returning calls promptly is equally important, according to Rathgeber. "I return all calls within fifteen minutes of receipt, and I always try to do the hardest ones first. Sometimes the surprise factor enters in, and, even if the person called with the intention of chewing me out, he's so surprised that I called back immediately that it winds up being a friendly conversation."

Reminded that not everybody has the Rolodex to lead to the person in charge, Rathgeber says, "Well, then you need to find out who *does* have the necessary contacts. Forget about e-mail. Use the telephone. It's so much more useful to call somebody on the phone, because it's harder to put a caller off. Also, your determination will come across over the phone. If you try to put the same message across in an e-mail, it might be offensive. Besides, with e-mail, the person you're trying to persuade can always hit the 'Delete' button."

Vast bureaucracies feature layer after layer of employees. Rathgeber reiterates that it does no good to talk to the wrong person. "After you find out who the decision maker is," he advises, "apply what I call my John-the-Baptist method; always send someone in to prepare the way. If you're trying to navigate through bureaucracy, you need to ask around until you find a person who is friends with the decision maker, somebody he listens to. When you're trying to do good work, there's always someone who's willing to help you. It's just a matter of finding that person."

After you've found the person responsible for what you're trying to accomplish, Rathgeber believes, you need to double-check everything. "If the person who's responsible didn't get the job accomplished, then you have to go over his or her head. It's an absolute fact that a bureaucrat will never buck up. He or she may get utterly furious at you for going over his head, but he won't risk getting fired over it. In the end, a bureaucrat will do as he or she is told."

He cites an example. "One time a city employee decided he was not going to issue a clearing permit for me. He just dug in his heels. But I knew that if we didn't complete the clearing for a subdivision in a timely manner, we'd be in violation of a federal law. After reminding this fellow of this fact several times, we finally went over his head. When he found out, he became livid. 'Why did you go over my head?' he demanded. 'Because you weren't doing your job,' was my reply. 'We had only three days to clear that land before the birds returned to their habitat. If we'd waited, we'd have been in violation of federal law.'"

When dealing with people in large organizations, Rathgeber assesses what he calls their "bug level." He explains, "Sometimes you have to determine what a person's bug level is. Recently, for example, we had an attorney who wouldn't return my attorney's calls. Finally my lawyer said, 'I guess I'm going to have to turn you loose, Dick.' With that, I called the lawyer's office every hour on the hour, and I kept repeating to his secretary that I *really* needed to talk to her boss, or rather my attorney needed to talk to him. I explained that we were trying to comply with the law on a development project, and we needed to confer. Of course, the secretary had no choice but to answer the phone whenever it rang. That was her job. After three hours of this, the lawyer finally called my attorney and said, 'Please tell Rathgeber not to call me anymore. He is driving my secretary absolutely nuts. Call him off, and I'll send you the information you want.' We had found his bug level. Perfect!

"If you do this, obviously you can't be overly concerned about whether you are offending people. I look at it this way. All I'm really doing is helping these bureaucrats do their job!"

Rathgeber has been known to use these tactics on his friends' projects as well as his own. According to one friend and former neighbor, "If Dick is in your corner, things start happening."

To illustrate, Dick tells a story about his friend Jim Lozier: "Jim and Della Lozier had been our neighbors, and Sara and I often traveled with them. As you know, Austin is known as a 'green city,' which means that recycling is very important to people here. Well, on one of our foreign trips with the Loziers, I noticed that Jim kept calling back home. I'd overhear him asking whether 'the sample had been approved yet.' I was curious about what kind of deal he was working on, so after a few of these mysterious calls, I asked him about it. Jim explained that he had come up with a plan—and the equipment—for crushing used concrete. This would enable the concrete to be used again. The state highway department had approved the material for use as road base, but the City of Austin and Travis County, for some reason, balked at giving their approval. Re-using concrete instead of putting it in the landfill sounded like a smart idea to me, from every point of view. As Jim and I talked about it on our trip, I could see the wisdom of his plan.

"It so happened that I had a subdivision that was just about ready for base, so as soon as we got home, I called the city manager's office and inquired about using this material. When, as expected, I was told the material had not been approved, I asked why. I explained I was just trying to be a responsible citizen. During that call, I learned that Jim had phoned on the matter again just the day before. He had been told that it would be three or four weeks before this city employee would have time to look at a sample. I just kept asking questions. Then I made a couple of calls to people higher up in the chain of command. In the end, my telephone calls created enough of a stir that the very next day this same employee was frantically calling Jim and asking him to bring over the sample. He said he didn't know what was going on up at City Hall, but he needed that sample right now! He was about four levels below the city manager, so there's no telling how much hair the story had on it by the time it reached him.

"Needless to say, the material was approved by the city for general usage, and it was subsequently approved at the

Travis County level. Today Mr. Lozier can sell all the crushed concrete he can produce. The material is being used for streets and subdivisions, and Mr. Lozier has a thriving business.

"This kind of bureaucratic snarl is completely unnecessary. You have to ask yourself what the holdup was. After all, what had the city and the county done with used concrete before? Well, they'd buried it in landfills, where it takes up space and will require centuries to decompose—if it ever does."

According to Rathgeber, bureaucrats come in all shapes and sizes. "The Lutheran Foundation of the Southwest is a church-related foundation that manages wills, bequests, and trusts," he says. "The foundation had been renting space in Austin, and they found it difficult to create an aura of permanence while operating out of a very cramped rented building. Leif Johnson, the number one Ford dealer in Austin and a member of the Lutheran Foundation Board, generously donated approximately five acres of land on the corner of U.S. Highway 290 and Giles Road for a new building for the foundation. We made plans to build, with most of the funds coming from Weimar Hein, a Chevrolet and Pontiac dealer in Fredericksburg who was chairman of the foundation board, Leif Johnson, and me.

"Everything was going fine until we went to the City of Austin and asked for water service. City officials said they could not let us have any water because the lines in place were completely overcommitted. I said, 'Oh, you'd let me have one little five-eighths-inch residential tap, wouldn't you?' They said, 'Okay, but that's all.' So we just put in a 3,000-gallon underground holding tank with an electric pressure pump. With that, we had all the water we would ever need, and we were able to complete the project on time."

Dick says entrepreneurs can't expect lower-level bureaucrats to do anything that is not strictly by the book. "That will never bring the results you want," he explains. "People who are lower in the chain of command are all about job protection. It's like the army. Very seldom will a bureaucrat get in trouble for doing too little, but he can get in lots of trouble if he sticks his neck out. When he does, he's infringed on somebody else's turf. In a bureaucracy, it's all about turf.

"Take the Salvation Army, which is actually a typical army. Turf protection is the primary issue. The best thing about my being on the national advisory board for nine years was that I got to know the people at the top. After that, if a project got stalled somewhere in the pipeline, I could find a way of breaking it loose.

"To illustrate: The Salvation Army's downtown shelter had approximately seventy-five women and children in the same building as the homeless men. If there was ever a recipe for disaster, that was it. Every officer was scared something bad was going to happen. As part of letting the City of Austin condemn the surplus land that the Salvation Army owned, our 'gentleman's agreement' with then Mayor Kirk Watson was that if we made nice on the land acquisition, he'd allow us to use the former Battered Women's Center building for the women and children in the Salvation Army shelter.

"In fact, the mayor went one better. He gave us a five-year lease on a $2 million building, spent $1 million renovating it, and gave us $1.4 million a year in operating money. A fantastic deal, wouldn't you say? But some mid-level bureaucrat in Atlanta attempted to turn the deal down on three different occasions because, he said, it violated the Salvation Army policy of not running a program on leased land. Their policy is always to own the land. Never mind that the future of seventy-five women and children was at stake.

"I found their position untenable, so I called the retired national commander, who was a good friend of mine, and I outlined the situation to him. I asked him for advice. 'Well,' he replied, 'the whole board in Atlanta has to give anybody a public hearing if he or she requests it. If the Salvation Army turns a deal down, any citizen can request such a hearing before the full board.' I immediately called Atlanta and said, 'I'm coming to talk to you about this deal. Please put me on the agenda. Also, I'd appreciate your having someone meet my plane.'

"Someone in Atlanta phoned me the next day saying I didn't need to come. So I waited a few days and nothing happened. I called again, asking to be put on the agenda. Again the following day, I received a call saying that I didn't need to come, because they were going to go ahead with the deal. This scenario recurred several times, and each time the officers in Atlanta would go around the back door, and inform the City of Austin that they were withdrawing their application to use that land. They didn't want to tell me this, so I was never notified directly. When they were talking to me, they would say everything was going through, but then they would tell the city they were withdrawing their request to use the land and building for the facility. This little dance kept being repeated.

"Eventually the application was submitted. However, the city required that a $1,000 cashier's check accompany the application—and no check came from Atlanta. The assistant city manager called me and said, 'The Salvation Army didn't put a check in here. What are you going to do?' Fortunately, with a cashier's check, anybody can be the remitter. I had a friendly banker who was willing to give me a cashier's check dated the previous day, so I zipped downtown with it, and that's how we managed to open the facility.

"I didn't know whether the Salvation Army's failure to send the check was passive-aggressive or just an oversight, but I didn't have time to worry about it. If I hadn't taken the check down immediately, the city would've had to throw the whole application out. The way I look at it, if you're sure you're doing the right thing, you just have to be willing to stick your neck out. After all, this one program benefiting homeless women and children could be worth $50 or $60 million to the Salvation Army over time."

Getting things done this way illustrates Rathgeber's claim that he's a D8 Dozer. He knows he probably offends people from time to time, but he doesn't care as long as his actions are necessary for one of his causes.

"I can't say it too many times. When you're dealing with a bureaucracy, assume nothing. Stay in close touch with all the players, check and double-check every detail, and don't waste your time worrying about whether people think you're nagging. Be willing to risk people's wrath. Who cares? Who else is going to advocate for the homeless, the wounded, the hungry? Even the Salvation Army, with all the good it does, needs prodding from time to time."

Apparently the Salvation Army hasn't been overly offended by Rathgeber's tactics. The church has awarded him all three of its awards: the Others Award, the Distinguished Auxiliary Service Award, and the William Booth Award. Research indicates he is the only civilian in history to have received all three.

The love goes both ways. Rathgeber says, "The Salvation Army has the same human frailties as any other large bureaucracy, but it's still the nation's number one charity. They absolutely do the best job of ministering to that segment of society on the very bottom of the socio-economic scale, the people who really have no one to advocate for them. And the Salvation Army provides this service with the lowest overhead. No wonder they are ranked America's foremost charity. Even though I have been frustrated with them at times, I remain one of their most ardent supporters."

## Sommer Elementary School

When building roads, Rathgeber is committed to considering the topography as well as what effect a new street will have on all surrounding land. On one occasion, such considerations gave him the chance to pay tribute to a dear friend. He tells the story:

"Sometimes city planners seem to think that roads and streets are just lines on paper. When we were developing Avery Ranch, for example, a very nice city planner from Cedar Park decided that Howard Lane needed to be extended through the most beautiful portion of the land. Trying to talk her out of this proved useless, so I decided to go about things in another way.

"To digress a little: Patsy and John Sommer are the definition of salt-of-the-earth people. They were our fellow members at St. Martin's Lutheran Church, and I'm telling you, sometimes you might have thought Patsy was clergy, because she was involved in so many things. She and I were mutually simpatico, perhaps because she, too, was the child of a Lutheran minister. Anyway, she had a razor-sharp wit and could deflate a person in a second. Unfortunately, Patsy had a long-running heart ailment, and in the late 1990s, she passed away. I wanted to commemorate this wonderful woman, so I asked John what he thought about naming an elementary school for her. She was a professional educator, and she'd been an assistant superintendent in the Round Rock School District. John said he thought it would be wonderful to name a school for Patsy.

"Well, Mr. Gau was the superintendent of schools for the Round Rock Independent School District at that time, so I invited him and his business manager to go to lunch with me. Over our meal, I asked him what his policy was for naming schools. He went into this long, drawn-out procedure whereby a committee was appointed, the matter studied, a recommendation made to the school board, and a vote eventually taken. I said, 'Mr. Gau, let me tell you my idea. I'm sure you remember that Patsy Sommer was one of your former assistant superintendents.'

"'Oh, yes,' he replied. 'Everybody loved Patsy.'"

Dick then proceeded to explain to the superintendent that he owned forty percent of the school site that the school district was hoping to acquire on Avery Ranch Road—which, by odd coincidence, was exactly where Howard Lane was supposed to come through. "I said I was willing to donate that land to the school district in exchange for their naming the elementary school for Patsy Sommer.

"'Oh, come to think of it,' Mr. Gau said, 'we don't need a committee.'"

Later the city planner for Cedar Park approached Dick again about extending Howard Lane. He replied, "Oh, you'll have to talk to the Round Rock ISD about that, because I no longer own that land."

Rathgeber believes that one agency will never interfere

in the business of another agency. "After that, the proposed extension of Howard Lane vanished," he says, concluding the story, "and the Patsy Sommer Elementary School held its grand opening on August 11, 2008."

## Helping Hand Home for Children and Shoal Creek Hospital

"I had a call from Kay McHorse, who happens to be the wife of my primary physician. When your doctor's wife calls, you listen. The Helping Hand Home for Children is a home for neglected and abused younger boys and girls. It is located on 38th Street just east of Guadalupe in Austin. It has a very small campus and has added to its site as surrounding properties became available. The last piece of property the home needed, which was right in the middle of their land, was a twelve-unit apartment house owned by the Texas Department of Mental Health and Mental Retardation. In 2004, this building was being used to house refugees from Hurricane Katrina. The Helping Hand children were within ten feet of the building, which was not ideal.

"When she called, Mrs. McHorse asked me if I would be willing to help Helping Hand buy that property. I agreed to do so, but when I investigated, I found out the property was owned by MHMR. I didn't know anybody in that organization. Using my John-the-Baptist process, I called my friend Fred Butler, who was involved with most local nonprofits. He was happy to set up a luncheon for me with David Evans, head of MHMR.

"At the luncheon, Mr. Evans agreed to take the issue up with his board, which subsequently settled on an appraised sales price of $520,000. At the end of the conversation, though, Mr. Evans pulled a Columbo. Remember how the television character used to say, 'Oh, there's just one more thing'? Well, David Evans said, 'What I really need are ten emergency psychiatric beds. We do not have beds for emergency psychiatric patients.'

"I asked him why he did not contact Seton Hospital, which owned a psychiatric hospital called Shoal Creek Hospital. 'They won't even talk to me,' he said. 'Let me be sure I understand you correctly,' I said. 'You would be willing to put this $500,000 into creating a special emergency facility for a minimum of ten psychiatric beds.'

"'Yes, I would do that,' he replied, and I told him I would see what I could do.

"I called Seton CEO Charles Barnett's office and requested a meeting with him and Jesus Garza for the purpose of discussing 'space modifications.' I added that I had money. Barnett's secretary called back within thirty minutes with a lunch appointment for three days later. They had reserved a room at the Headliners Club.

"At the lunch, towards the end of the meal, we finally got around to business. I said, 'I want to discuss ten emergency psychiatric beds with you.' At this time they were in the process of vacating the old children's hospital at Brackenridge. I had done my homework, and I knew that they absolutely did not want these beds at Brackenridge, because they had already committed the space. I saw the two of them exchange anxious glances and I said, 'No, no, no. You have it all wrong. I'm not asking for these beds to be at Brackenridge. MHMR wants them to be at Shoal Creek Hospital.

"'Oh, well, that's a different matter,' said Barnett.

"Jesus Garza said, 'Would you like for me to take this

to the Travis County Healthcare District and ask for operating funds as well?'

"I was delighted for him to do this, and plans were made to modify a whole wing of Shoal Creek, which meant that instead of ten beds they got sixteen. It was a wonderful solution for the mentally ill of Travis County, and also a typical example of how agencies often fail to communicate with each other.

"The money MHMR got from the sale of the apartment house went into remodeling the wing of Shoal Creek Hospital, and what started out as a simple real estate deal wound up providing emergency psychiatric resources for mentally ill people."

## Seton Hospital Board of Directors

Dick fondly recalls his time on the Seton Hospital board of directors. "Serving with all those nuns was just a hoot," he says. "I was not Catholic, so I was completely irreverent. I remember when Seton got ready to expand, they became embroiled in a vicious zoning fight with the Brykerwoods Neighborhood Association. That association joined forces with St. Andrew's Episcopal School, and the two groups together equaled a formidable opposition to the hospital's expansion plans.

"In the middle of all that, I got a call from Sandy Gottesman suggesting we meet for coffee. When we met and talked, it became apparent that what St. Andrew's really wanted was room for one more classroom building. I suggested that Seton could possibly sell them a couple of lots at appraised value and give them a year to pay so that they would have time to do fund-raising. The deal was that, at the same time Seton gave them an option to buy these lots, the school would turn a letter over to Seton, giving full support to Seton's zoning application. That broke the back of the opposition, and Seton got the zoning that they needed. St. Andrew's later built a new classroom building."

Some time later, Seton Hospital needed to expand. The decision was made to build a facility in the northwest part of town. "When they got ready to expand," Dick says, "they took a large delegation to the headquarters of the Daughters of Charity in St. Louis to get approval for another location. Since I was on the board at the time, I was asked to go along. Our group took all kinds of accountants, flow chart experts, and demographers with them, and when they started their presentation, they were literally putting those nuns at headquarters to sleep."

Dick asked to be the final speaker. "I got up and said it looked like to me that choosing a new location for a hospital was like killing hogs. The nuns jerked their heads up and listened. I told them my dad had been a Lutheran minister who always served in rural parishes. Whenever one of his parishioners killed a hog, he would bring the preacher some meat. Well, one time one of Dad's neighbor preachers was brought a whole bunch of pigs' feet. The preacher was polite and said, 'Thank you very much, but if it's all the same to you I believe I'd like to eat a little higher on the hog.' The nuns roared with laughter as I concluded, 'Nobody wants to build a hospital in south or southeast Austin because there are no pork chops there.'

"For years afterward, every time I saw a nun who had been at the meeting, she would ask whether I was still killing hogs."

Dick recalls another of the board meetings he attended. "At the end of the meeting, we were saying good-bye to

Sister Peggy, a younger nun who was leaving the order. I said I always worried about Sister Peggy, because she drove back and forth to San Antonio, sometimes late at night, by herself. One time she ran out of gas about a quarter of a mile from a gas station where the attendant sat in a bullet-proof cage. The sister walked up to the cage, explained she had run out of gas, and asked whether the attendant had a can she could use to get some gas. He said no, they didn't have anything like that. Then the sister remembered that she was just coming from the hospital, where she had been helping replace some equipment. For that reason, she had an old bedpan in the car. She went back to the car, retrieved the bedpan, and bought a gallon of gas. As she was pouring the gas into her tank, a couple of good ol' boys were just passing by, heading home from the bar. When they saw what she was doing, one turned to the other and said, 'Now, brother, that's faith!'

"Some of those nuns are still among my best friends," Dick concludes, smiling.

# The Ripple Effect

Sometimes when people come together for a good cause, it's remarkable the momentum that can build. A force seems to come from outside the range of any one individual, and its extent can be astonishing. One connection leads to another; one effort builds and gains strength until a power nobody could have predicted has coalesced. Such is what happened with the effort of several Austinites in the Central American country of Honduras.

And when Dick Rathgeber joined forces with these people, the results were even more far-reaching.

It all started in October 1998, when a small team from Austin's Tarrytown United Methodist Church was in Central America to build a library in north central Honduras, a rural village called Dos Rios. They were there through the auspices of Honduras Outreach, a mission group based in Atlanta.

One man with a long-standing interest in Honduras, Jim Morriss, was among them. As it happened, the devastating Hurricane Mitch hit Honduras while they were there. Jim takes up the story: "At that time, I was serving on the board of Honduras Outreach, and my wife and I were the only ones in our group who spoke Spanish. When the storm hit, our Honduran contact came to me and said that mudslides had started. 'We need to get you out of the country,' he said.

"We were in the middle of basic construction, so I replied, 'Well, when the guys come in for lunch, we'll consult.'

"'No!' he exclaimed. 'We go now!'"

Before they knew it, the Texans were in vans heading for Juticalpa. En route, they began to grasp the extent of Hurricane Mitch's devastation. "We had to be dragged through mudslides with a tractor," Morriss recalls. "We spent that night in Juticalpa, and the next day we got to Tegucigalpa, where we were stuck for five days. During that time, we continued to hear news of the havoc wreaked by the storm. We were staying in a four-star hotel where there was food and water, but thousands upon thousands of poor Honduran people were not so lucky. Immediately we all pitched in to pack food for rescuers and help distribute clothing and water. It became clear that the storm had left complete wreckage in its wake."

After the group finally got home on November 3, Jim and Annette Morriss remained haunted by what they had seen in this largest—and poorest—country in Central America. "Shortly after we returned to Austin," Morriss says, "I received a call from a man named John Ellett. I didn't know John, but he had gotten my name from a man who had been on our team in Honduras. John explained that he was a member of Riverbend [Church] and that as he had been hearing about the havoc in Honduras, he felt a compulsion to do something to help. 'I don't know anything about Honduras,' he said, 'but I really want to set up some system of aid. I don't have the first idea how to start. Will you help me?'

"I told him I had a long-standing commitment to the people of Honduras and that I'd be glad to help if I could."

About a month after Hurricane Mitch, Jim and Annette Morriss went back to Honduras, and as they toured through Juticalpa, they saw that the bridge through town had washed out. "All the shanties, where the poorest of the poor had lived, were gone. As we wandered through the area, we ran into the mayor of Juticalpa, who said, 'We have inventoried the people who lived along the river here. There are sixty-five families, and they've lost everything. A landowner in the area has donated land to relocate them, but they have no resources. There's no way for them to move.'

"Immediately I thought of John Ellett and his desire to help. 'This sounds like a ready-made project,' I said to Annette. When we got back from the trip, I called John and told him about the land that had been donated and the need for funds to help the homeless families move. He said, 'Let's go down there.' So we did, just the two of us. We'd been advised to get in touch with the Rotary Club, which of course was made up of business leaders with an interest in the community. We were readily received by the Rotarians, and they immediately hosted a fish fry for us at their building. Then they showed us the land that had been donated for the sixty-five families. As we talked to these businesspeople about our providing funds, and their providing construction and management, they began to comprehend that we were serious. John and I had a firm feeling of confidence in these town leaders: owner of a car battery factory, Coca-Cola bottler, tailor, auto parts store owner, dentist, banker. These men made up the intelligentsia of the community.

"That afternoon we visited one Rotarian's farm, where the group held another fish fry in our honor. It was a party, the warmest kind of camaraderie, and we enjoyed their hospitality. Throughout the gathering, I was translating for John, who, although a gregarious person, was at a loss because he didn't speak Spanish.

"By the end of that day, I told the president of the Rotary that we were prepared to sign an agreement to outline what they would promise to do and what we would promise to do in order to relocate these sixty-five families. Marco Antonio Montes was the Rotary president's name, and he convened a formal meeting of the board right then and there. We agreed to provide funds, partnering with Honduras Outreach, which already had its 501(c)(3) designation, as well as an established office in Juticalpa with a secretary, an accountant, and a relationship with a bank there. The Hondurans, through the Rotary Club, agreed to buy materials and provide construction and management. We gave the effort the name Austin Helps Honduras and signed the agreement, which was really just a letter of intent, not legally binding. But we were quite serious. I said to John, 'Okay, let's go home now, and get the money.' We were only in Honduras for two days on that trip, so we accomplished a lot in a little time."

Soon after the two men returned to Austin, John Ellett arranged to talk about Austin Helps Honduras on a local Saturday morning television show. He asked Jim Morriss to accompany him. They had only three minutes to make their pitch. Ellett told the audience that the needy people had been identified, the land for relocation had been donated, and that he believed simple houses could be built for $2,500 per family. "The Rotary Club had suggested we build duplexes," Morriss adds, "which meant that we could shelter two families for $5,000."

As it happened, Dick Rathgeber was watching television the morning John and Jim were making their pitch. Dick remembered Jim Morriss from when they shared a barrack when both were in the army, in 1955. Morriss says, "I hadn't been home from that interview for thirty minutes when the phone rang. It was Dick."

Morriss reports the following conversation:

Dick: "Jim, can you do what you said you were going to do?"

Jim: "I think we can. I have experience through my church, so I know Honduras. Also, I speak Spanish."

Dick, in his distinctive drawl: "Well, I'm going to he'p you."

Jim: "What kind of help did you have in mind?"

Dick: "Ross Perot says, 'I like to see where my dollar goes.' I feel the same way. I'll give you $5,000 and you go down there and build one of those houses. Bring me a picture and if I like it, I'll give you some more money."

Jim: "We're hoping to move a little faster than that, Dick, but thanks. We'd sure like your help."

Meanwhile, John Ellett was busily raising money. He was an independent marketing consultant for high-tech companies, and he had formerly worked for Dell. He put $25,000 into the project. A former Dell colleague added another $25,000. John went to his pastor at Riverbend Church, Gerald Mann, and the church put in an additional $75,000. In addition, Austin Helps Honduras had received another couple of calls after the television in-

terview, so John was able to send something a little shy
of $150,000 to Honduras Outreach, to be drawn on by
the Rotary Club of Juticalpa. This all took place in January,
and construction started immediately.

"By April of that year, Dick went with John and me to
dedicate the first eight units," says Morriss. "He also
brought his pastor, Sam Zumwalt. At the dedication ceremony were all sorts of representatives from the community:
the assistant mayor, police chief, the president of the
*damnificados*, which is the local name for the homeless
people who would be living in the new *colonia*. The word
means 'the injured, or those who suffered.' In all, a group
of perhaps forty people attended the dedication, and already we had a waiting list of another sixteen families. The
president of the *damnificados* said, 'It's hard to believe
that we had our first conversation about this project in
January, and now, three months later, our dream has come
true.'

"During the ceremony, Dick poked me and said, 'Ask
him how much they have in the budget to get water to these
houses. I want it in the public record.' I asked his question,
but the mayor's representative said he wasn't sure. Dick responded, 'Ask him what difference it would make if half the
materials were paid for.' The fellow replied, 'Well, that
would help.' He was prevaricating, of course. He wasn't in
a position to commit. So Dick said, through my translation,
'What if ALL the materials were paid for?' Naturally the
Hondurans liked that idea.

"Dick said, 'Well, have him send me a list of exactly
what is needed. When I get that list, I'll pay for the materials.' Dick just couldn't see building these houses without
water. The people would have had to hike a good distance
to the river, and that didn't seem right to him."

THE *COLONIA* THAT THE TEXANS' MONEY built is known as *Colonia Solidaridad* and, although Dick didn't know it yet, his commitment to these Hondurans had just begun.

As promised, he supplied the materials to pipe water to the houses. As it turned out, it was a straight shot—about two kilometers—from the *colonia* to the water system in Juticalpa. Through his city engineer, the mayor proposed laying ten-inch pipes for the new water system. Dick countered that four-inch pipes would be adequate to serve this little community of five hundred.

"What Dick hadn't realized, though, was that people all along the way would hook into the system," explains Morriss. "Juticalpa is actually a municipality, comparable to a county in the United States. In each municipality, the largest town is designated as the seat of municipal government—but there are a number of smaller towns within the municipality. The whole area where we were working is rural. Hondurans call it the Wild West of their country. Many people there carry pistols in their belts and settle disagreements with machetes. The entire municipality of Juticalpa is about the size of Travis County, and when all was said and done, the water system Dick supplied benefited more than two thousand people. That's why ten-inch pipes were necessary."

By that time the people of Juticalpa had figured out that this group from Austin was quite serious about helping them, and when the Texans came to visit, they began to be followed by television, radio, and newspaper reporters.

After the water system was in, Dick wanted the people to have electricity, as well as a workable sewage system—and he paid for, and oversaw, these major projects himself. But the needs in a country like Honduras are never-ending.

For example, during one trip to Juticalpa, Rathgeber was trying to get the electric system up and running. He and others from Austin Helps Honduras were in the mayor's office for that reason, but a few days earlier there had been a deluge of rain that had done even more damage to the infrastructure of the municipality than Hurricane Mitch had. The sewer system was backed up, and sanitary conditions were deplorable. There was a cholera epidemic just waiting to happen. The Hondurans had another major crisis on their hands.

Jim Morriss recalls that the mayor showed the Americans a video of the recent flood damage. "He was asking us to help in any way we could. They had no way of clearing the sewage system, which was completely dysfunctional. The mayor said there was a large drainage system pump in a city some three hundred miles away that had the capability to clear the system. This was a specialized machine, self-propelled, that operated from a truck. However, it cost $1,000 a day to rent, and there was no money for that in the mayor's budget. Before we left that day, Dick had agreed to cover the cost of renting the pump for ten days, and with that, the officials were able to rehabilitate the storm sewers for the city."

As soon as Dick agreed to rent the pump, the mayor and his staff said, "Let us show you another subdivision."

So the group went to a nearby *colonia* that had been built by the Italian Red Cross and others. It included forty nice houses—but no sewer, no electricity. "Dick was outraged," Morris says. "He asked, 'Why didn't the Italian Red Cross take care of this?' and the mayor replied, 'Well, they don't do this. They don't have the skills or money. The houses are needed, but nobody can live here because there's no infrastructure.' So those nice houses were standing empty while hundreds of local people were homeless. The Juticalpa city engineer was conducting the tour that day, and of course members of the press were following us. Dick showed the city engineer how the whole thing needed to be set up. Finally the Honduran engineer turned to me and said, 'Will you tell this guy I'm a graduate engineer and I know sh*t runs downhill?' Dick laughed, and on the spot he offered $50,000 to provide the needed infrastructure."

It was on that same trip that another pressing need came to light. Explains Morriss, "We had completed all the houses for Colonia Solidaridad, and we traveled to Honduras for a celebratory dinner with the Rotary. I noticed a man I hadn't seen before, who was having an animated conversation with one of the Rotarians. When we were introduced, I learned he was the city fire chief. He told me that one of the city's urgent needs was a new fire truck. I passed this information on to Dick, who said, 'No, no. We're not in the fire truck business.' So I told the man that, regrettably, our resources were committed.

"We completed our trip and soon returned to Texas. A week or so later, I received a call from Dick. Much to my surprise, he said, 'Jim, I just bought me a fire truck. How are we going to get it down to Honduras?' Without fanfare, he had done some research and learned that in the United States, after fire trucks are ten years old, city fire departments refurbish them for sale to rural towns.

"Immediately I called our representative in Honduras, who told me that a new law had passed saying that no vehicle more than ten years old could be imported into the country.

"I reported this to Dick, who thought that law didn't make much sense. A little more research revealed that the president of the Honduran Congress happened to be from

Juticalpa. After that, working through the Rotary Club in Juticalpa, we literally got the law amended to state that no vehicle older than ten years could be imported into the country *except for* ambulances, fire trucks, etc. That's how Dick managed to provide them with a good-as-new fire truck."

Not long after that, Dick and Jim went down to see the town's new fire truck. Almost immediately, Dick was approached about buying the town an ambulance. Their one ambulance barely ran, and the need for a new one was undeniable. But Dick said, through Jim, "No, no, no. We just bought you a fire truck."

Jim says, "Of course, Dick had already done so much for the people of Juticalpa. I thought the idea of a new ambulance was a closed question. But when he got back to Texas, Dick did some more research (while picking up a new car he had bought), and he bought a new chassis for an ambulance. He thought this would provide exactly what they needed in Juticalpa. As with the fire truck, he had it shipped to the Port of Cortes, then driven the several hundred miles to Juticalpa. Dick had more fun on subsequent trips, as he went down to see 'his' fire truck and ambulance."

Something about the people of Honduras had touched Dick in a deep way. He thought about their lively spirit and the trials they faced every day, just trying to survive. He wished more people knew about them. Because he believes that helping people who so desperately need help leads to a more meaningful life for the giver, he finds himself wanting to pass that on.

On his first fact-finding mission to Honduras, Dick had taken his pastor, Sam Zumwalt. Pastor Zumwalt was impressed with what he saw there, and when he returned, he talked to one of his parishioners, an artist named Bunny Oliver, about it. "Sam wanted to get the congregation involved in the *colonia*," Bunny recalls. "He talked to me about how beautiful the country was, and how he thought I would enjoy painting there. He told me I would love the children of the *colonia*. This is an example of how Dick changes lives with his philanthropy. He exposes one person to some glaring need, and that person talks about the experience to another, who then passes the enthusiasm on to another person, and on it goes. When I got back from that first trip to the *colonia*, I talked to Dick about it, and he was so excited that I had been there. He started encouraging me to do more. I'm not sure what he saw in me that could be useful, but something must have told him that I would get involved.

"As it happened, I had been to Italy with my husband until a few days before we left for Honduras on that initial trip. In fact, we got back from Europe on a Friday, and I left for Central America the following Wednesday. In doing so, I moved directly from opulence to poverty.

"I remember it well. We flew into Tegucigalpa, the capital of Honduras. From there, it's a three-and-a-half-hour drive to Julticalpa. I was not prepared, the next morning, to drive into the *colonia*. As I looked around me, I saw so much poverty. The air smelled bad. There was refuse in the streets, and people were ragged and sometimes homeless. But at the same time, we were surrounded by dozens of beautiful children, with eyes like melted chocolate that look at you with hope and joy. The people we met couldn't wait to show us their homes, which were, in fact, very modest. But they had running water! And by the end of that year, they had electricity. They were happy and proud.

"I guess we all do what we can. I am a painter, so I decided to paint what I saw there. I had brought my paints—oils—but I wasn't allowed to bring turpentine, so we went to a hardware store and bought what must be the roughest grade of turpentine in the world. I remember how it smelled up the vans. The children had never seen anybody paint. They would crowd around and watch me. I fell in love with those children, as does everyone who goes on one of our trips. They're so poor, and their bodies are dusty. They have no toys. Our bottles from bottled water were just treasures to them. They would make up games to play with these bottles. I found myself looking at these children and thinking, What are your dreams? Do you even know what there is to dream about?

"Juan Pablo Aguilera is the sole employee of Austin Helps Honduras. He makes our travel arrangements, coordinates our trips, keeps our records, and oversees our projects. On Saturday that week of my first trip, Juan Pablo needed to go back to his office, and I rode along with him. As I sat waiting for him to finish what he was doing, I happened to pick up a brochure describing how the government only pays for education through the sixth grade—and even that education is minimal. The government is so broke. I asked if I could have the brochure, thinking maybe we could use my paintings to raise money for scholarships."

When the Texans visit Honduras, they stay at a bed-and-breakfast called Villa San Andres. When the group returned to the B&B that day, the electricity had gone out—a common occurrence—so the group members moved outside to stay cool. "As we sat there, I told the others about my idea for providing scholarships for the children," Bunny says. "I showed them the brochure I'd found. Privately, I made the decision that when we got back to Austin I would paint ten paintings. I thought we could make limited-edition prints and  posters, as well as note cards. That way, people who couldn't afford an original painting might be able to afford a poster, or at least some cards."

The group came home, and a year later Austin Helps Honduras sponsored a fund-raiser at the Caswell House, a historic house in downtown Austin. "We raised $13,000," Bunny reports. "Afterward, I still had some paintings and other items left. Over the next twelve months, I sold them at art shows, and the total reached $30,000; we launched a scholarship program in February 2002 for the children of Colonia Solidaridad. We requested applications, and everybody who applied that first year got a scholarship. Each child had to have adequate grades, be a good citizen, and have a genuine desire to go to school. It had to be each child's own desire and not somebody else's. And of course, they all had to have a financial need.

"The scholarships were $400 apiece, and this amount covered all expenses, including fees, books, school supplies, uniforms, shoes, and transportation to and from school. It also included incidentals. The first year, nine scholarships were given for children to go to middle school, and five women received scholarships for a vocational sewing class.

"So this was my thrust when I first went to Honduras. By now, I've visited the area many times, and I know the kids. I know their names, and I've watched them grow up. Our purpose is not to change their culture, but to help them have a safer, healthier life, as well as some kind of job that will help them feed their families. We give the scholarship money equally to boys and girls, which is important, because when we go to Juticalpa, we see mainly women and children. Many men are in the U.S. or on farms, working.

"As I said, that first year, fourteen scholarships were awarded," Bunny says. "The next year we gave nineteen.

Seven were vocational, and the others were academic. One of the vocational programs was a cosmetology school. We gave one boy money to go to barber school for a year, and today he has a barber's chair in his home. Some women set up beauty salons in their homes. These people are moving up. We've even had three high school graduates through our program. I think of Alba, a little girl we started helping in 2002, who graduated from high school in 2006. You see, there are very few high school graduates in Juticalpa, and five young people from our program will graduate in 2008.

"As of now, we have given more than two hundred scholarships, with forty-three students attending school through our program in 2008. Most of the scholarships are provided now by people in the U.S., who sponsor one or more children for a year. It's very rewarding to see these students improve their lives and the lives of their children, and it's rewarding for me to see people generously sponsor children whom they may never meet. And of course, I owe the satisfaction of this work I'm doing to Dick Rathgeber. He also provided that opportunity for countless others who are now involved as sponsors of students. They, too, are blessed with the satisfaction of helping others. This is some of the most satisfying work I've ever done."

Today, Bunny Oliver is president of the board of Austin Helps Honduras. To date she has made eight trips to Colonia Solidaridad.

A FEW YEARS AGO, Chas Studor was an electrical engineer with a semiconductor physics background. "I'd been moving up through the ranks in chip design," he says. "I was the senior design manager for a billion-dollar unit for what is now Freescale. I had eight different design centers around the world, where we would design custom chips for large companies—all the automotive makers, etc. Since I was responsible for leading teams in, for example, Brazil, China, Japan, Taiwan, Germany, and India, I was often gone for a week at a time."

Chas first heard about the mission program in Central America when someone from his church, St. Martin's Lutheran, spoke about visiting Honduras. Chas decided to go on the next trip, mainly because it was so different from anything he had done before.

"When I went to Honduras with the group from church, I found the experience extremely moving," he recalls. "I was welcomed into the *colonia*, which was similar to communities I'd seen from the back of a limo or taxi in Third World countries I visited for work. But I'd had no connection to those communities.

"My trip was perhaps the third one for the group, so we were completely welcomed into this *colonia*. As we drove in, we were swarmed by people carrying banners in Spanish and English. The people had a list of our names, and one sign read, 'Welcome, Charles Studor.' People in our group already knew the villagers. Since I was new, I didn't know anybody, so I went off to a corner. Within minutes, I was surrounded by a swarm of little kids playing hand games. I didn't speak Spanish, so they used gestures to get me involved. One little girl with grimy hands held on to my leg. I felt like a member of the family. Before this, I would have been afraid even to get out of the car."

The first Sunday after he returned from that trip, Chas was approached by Dick at church. "How did you like what you saw in Honduras?" Dick asked him. Chas, who didn't know Dick well or have much idea about what Dick did for a living, replied that it had been interesting. "Well, I'd like to take you to lunch to talk about it," Dick said, and Chas gave a noncommittal nod.

Chas recalls, "I guess Dick had heard that the trip to Honduras was something I had enjoyed. We went to the church together, and I suppose I knew he'd helped some people out, but I didn't have an idea of him as different from anybody else at the church. When he asked me to lunch, I couldn't imagine what we had in common. But I looked at my calendar and found a date about three weeks out.

"When I got home and told my wife, Robin, about it, she said, 'So you told Dick Rathgeber that you MIGHT have time for him in three weeks? Don't you realize there are people who would give anything for a little of Dick's time?'"

The appointed day arrived, and Dick and Chas went to lunch at a Chinese restaurant. Chas and his wife, Robin Melvin, had twin boys who were then about five years old. The family was known around St. Martin's Lutheran Church because the twins had been premature and the family had been on the prayer list for weeks when the babies were newborns. By this time, though, the boys were healthy and thriving.

"At lunch, Dick started to talk," Chas says. "He asked me questions about my work and even more questions about my family. He was curious about the amount of traveling I was doing, given the fact that the boys were so young and my wife was a busy attorney. I explained that, as soon as I got on a plane, I'd figure out how to hit the ground running with my employees. Then I'd get home and the boys would want my attention. I was probably traveling one week a month, sometimes more, so I learned how to switch gears a day and a half before I switched time zones. I couldn't be bothered with jet lag. I just learned to live in my head in the coming time zone. Needless to say, this took a lot of psychic energy."

Rathgeber listened patiently to Chas's description of his busy life. "Then he started to talk about his values," Chas recalls. "He said, 'It sounds like you have been working hard at being successful.' Well, I couldn't deny that. I'd been promoted to a position as high as I could go as a designer. I had a coach who was working for me and he said, 'You're on track to be the top technical person.' Now I was there. I suddenly realized I didn't need to be more successful, and besides, I'd figured out that higher success in my field meant I would be in meetings all day, or on planes, or deciding whom to fire.

"Dick said, 'Chas, I want you to remember a simple formula. S + S = C. Success plus significance equals contentment. If you're successful but you're not making a significant contribution to the world, you'll never be content.' That really struck me. By the end of that lunch, I had decided to have more conversations with this Dick Rathgeber."

Chas left in a pensive mood that day. He found himself thinking deeply about his life and its direction. "I realized my ego was driving me," he says now. "I was concerned with what I thought of myself, how I measured my success in my field, and what others thought of me. But Dick was right. I didn't feel that my life was significant. Over the next few weeks, he and I had a number of conversations. He talked to me about family, about marriage. I was crazy about my boys, but the fact was, Robin's sister was caring for them and managing our household."

Quite soon, the men's conversations turned to Dick's

charitable efforts. "He asked me what I was doing about giving," Chas says. "I told him we gave a little, but that I didn't even write the checks. When he asked what I got out of that, I had to be honest. 'Not much,' I replied. The fact was, Robin and I had always made contributions—to the church, to this good cause or that one—but they had always seemed to me like just another bill to pay. I hadn't given them much attention.

"Then one day Dick set forth his belief that a person should 'follow the money.' Asked what he meant, he explained that if you're donating to a cause, you should go there. Be on the board. Volunteer. The next time I went to Honduras with him and Jim Morriss, I saw what he meant. They'd built all these houses in the *colonia*, but they'd had septic tanks that didn't work, and there was sewage in the streets. Dick wanted to solve the problem. Anybody else would have just written a check, but Dick said, 'Let's talk to the mayor.' And sure enough, we found somebody who works these deals in Honduras. When he's trying to help solve a problem, Dick makes it a point to meet the people, talk to them, and find the best solution. He hires people and then follows up to be sure the work has been done, and done right. After he figures out what the need is, he monitors the situation from then on. He gets such joy out of following the money."

A year later, Chas's company was undergoing a restructuring, and he decided to leave professional life for a while. Through these conversations with Dick, he had come to realize that he wanted to spend more time with his sons and wife and that he did want to make a contribution in the world. "Soon after I left my company," he says, "I decided I wanted to build a school for those children in the *colonia*. Of course, I had no idea how to build a school. I had never done anything like that. But Dick said, 'Chas, if you go down there and figure out how to build a school, I'll give you matching funds.'"

Studor knew that if he was going to build a school, he would need help, so he headed to Central America and looked up the Honduran Red Cross, which agreed to help. "After I figured out that the Red Cross was the way to go," he says, "I took pictures of schools they had built in other parts of Honduras. In the *colonia*, six grades of between 150 and 170 students were being held in one room. The staff included a principal and three teachers. Excited, I showed the principal a photo of the sort of school we wanted to build. To my surprise, she just glared at me and said, through a translator, 'Why are you showing me this? It's impossible for us. This is mean. Please go away.' She couldn't even *imagine* such a nice place for these children. After all, these were the poorest of the poor, the *damnificados*. Nobody expected anything, as they had been lied to so many times by local officials.

"In the end, though, we did build them a school. I got to help design it and oversee the whole deal. I made a lot of phone calls, sent e-mails, and made another four trips. When the school was opened, the principal, who hadn't been able to fathom such a building only a year earlier, handed me a list of things she needed, and it included a performing arts center! Looking into her appreciative eyes, I began to understand the whole $S + S = C$ equation. The minister of education of the State of Olancho has called that school the best school the Red Cross has built in the state."

Chas sometimes wonders what made Dick prod him as he did. When Dick is asked that question, he replies, "Well, I just didn't think Chas was as happy as he could be."

For his part, Chas assumes Dick saw in him the ability

to manage managers of managers. "That's what I had done in my professional life," he says. "Dick mentored me to the point where I felt confident—after watching him negotiate the sewer deal—that I could build a school."

Chas's entire life changed. Thanks to his supportive wife, Robin, today Chas is a stay-at-home dad who gets to walk his kids to school each day. He's also the chair of the board of the Austin Children's Shelter; chair of the board of St. Martin's preschool; a member of the advisory board of the Salvation Army—on the strategic planning committee, mainly concerned with the Kroc Center; and of course on the board of Austin Helps Honduras.

The work of this relatively small group of people in Honduras just keeps rippling outward. For example, a young woman who grew up in St. Martin's, Karen Pitcher, is CEO of an extended-care hospital in San Antonio, and she has conducted three medical mission trips to Colonia Solidaridad. Through her efforts people throughout Juticalpa, people who had never seen a doctor before have been treated. In those three trips, as many as 4,500 people have been seen.

Jim Morriss says, "Rathgeber's financial contributions to the people of Juticalpa amount to just under a quarter of a million dollars. But even more importantly, he continues to pull other people in. Here's another example. After he helped broker the move of the children's hospital to the Mueller development, Charles Barnett of Seton was grateful. He said, 'Dick, what's a charity we can make a contribution to in your honor?'

"'Well,' says Dick, 'how much did you have in mind?'

"'About five thousand,' Barnett answered.

"'Let's make it ten,' said Dick. 'I happen to know about a subdivision in Honduras, a different one, run by the

Catholic Church. The people there have to walk up the hill and buy water a bucket at a time. A well in Honduras costs ten thousand.

"'Are you in?'"

# Be a Mentor

Terry Mitchell is an Austin businessman and lawyer who owns a development company called Momark. He first got into the business when, in 1991, he served as legal counsel for Milburn, a development company. "I started as general counsel for Milburn. Before long, I realized I was more interested in the development part of the business than the legal part. In 1993, Continental homes of Phoenix bought the company, and that's when I was asked to take over the land department. For thirteen years, I did that work. In 1999, we were bought by D.R. Horton—now the first or second biggest developer in the country.

"In 2003, I decided to go out on my own. That's when I started Momark. As I was working for Continental, I learned how to serve a constituency and offer, for example, great parks and a broader range of housing. We began really expanding what we were doing. I always wanted to do good work, but the truth is, I needed a model. Who was doing the sort of work that mattered? I think I wondered even before I could articulate the question.

"I first heard of Dick Rathgeber in 1982, when I read in the newspaper that he had donated that land for the

Salvation Army. Who in his right mind would give away $3 million? I figured he had to have an angle. No right-thinking businessman just throws that kind of money away. There had to be more to it. But what?

"Over the next few years, I kept reading about Dick giving away money, giving away land, just making all these contributions to charities around town and even throughout the state. I simply couldn't figure this guy out. I was suspicious of him—but that's because I was looking at things from a secular point of view."

Eventually, in 1997, the two men met and became partners in developing the Avery Ranch subdivision. "Even there, I was flummoxed by Dick," Mitchell recalls. "I mean, we had been trying to buy that property for the longest time, but we were getting nowhere. There were three factions of the same family who owned the land, and we couldn't come to agreement. Then Dick comes in, and all of a sudden he has control of two-thirds of the land. I remember walking into my boss's office and telling him that Rathgeber had control of that land we had been trying so hard to procure. A few days later, Dick and I sat down for a meeting, and Dick said, 'Tell me about yourself.' That was different. He didn't start with the bottom line. He seemed more interested in who I was as a person.

"I told him I was trying to serve people, and he asked me how my career had started. I mentioned that I had worked at a downtown bank, for a fellow named Jack Collins. I told him Jack had become a mentor to me. Well, Dick called Jack the next day, and he asked for the lowdown on me. Jack spoke well of me, and the next day Dick called me. 'Let's do a deal,' he said. It was clear that he was interested in my character, and that if he didn't think I had integrity, he simply wouldn't work with me."

It wasn't a slam dunk from there, though. There were still

details to be ironed out. "We ended up working it out that our company would buy raw land from Dick, and he would put up the remaining forty percent of investment funds," says Mitchell. "Our idea was to build a planned community with two separate ownerships. I remember Dick said, 'You talk price, I'll talk terms. You talk terms, I'll talk price.' Because Dick wanted more money for the land than we wanted to pay, we worked out the terms. He thought his price was the market value, so he was very fair on the terms. Very flexible. Even so, it took us six months to come to agreement. We met and met. In all those meetings, I got to know him better. I really looked up to him for the way he handled himself as a businessman. Dick is the same age as my dad, so I guess you could say there's a father-son aspect to our relationship."

Eventually the two sides came to terms and Terry, thinking that was that, was ready to leave the table. He stood and extended his hand. "But Dick said, 'Oh, there's one more thing.' I'm thinking, What in the world? We've tied up the deal to build 2,600 houses. But Dick said, 'For every house you build, I want you to donate $100 to the charity of your choice, and I'll match it.' I had *never* heard of anything like that. I was amazed. We all just stared at him with our mouths open, and Dick said, 'I don't do business with people who aren't charitable.'

"As we agreed to his request, I did the math and realized that we had just given away $260,000 which, with his matching funds, would equal $520,000."

Mitchell believes the unusual thing about Dick is not only the way he does business, but also the effect he has on the people around him. "At the end of that year," Mitchell says, "we had sold 260 houses. My boss said, 'Okay, folks, we owe $26,000 to a charity. Who do you want to give it to?' We had a blast deciding. In the end, we gave it to John

Avery's wife's favorite charity, which was the Ronald McDonald House. I can't even describe the joy of that experience! It changed the way I do business."

In 2000, the two had worked together and known each other for three years. Terry was no longer suspicious of Dick, but he was still trying to understand what motivated him. "One day I was sitting at his house and he got a call. He left me alone in his living room. I noticed a big ol' family Bible sitting there, and I opened it. I saw his father's name, and that was the first time I found out his dad had been a Lutheran minister. Dick had never mentioned it. He is about as un-pious as they come, but that day it suddenly dawned on me. 'He's a Christian! He's trying to do God's will!'

"Dick has influenced everything I do. For example, I'm now involved in a project called Goodnight, Texas, which is northeast of Onion Creek and a mile east of I-35. It's an affordable-housing development, with units priced from the low $100,000s to $300,000, and as we sell those houses, three tenths of a percent of the sales price of every piece of real estate will go to a foundation to help enhance education. In perpetuity. This is a result of my knowing Dick Rathgeber."

Once Terry Mitchell asked Dick how he made the decision to do business with him in the first place, and to do so on a handshake. He's never forgotten Dick's answer: "If you trust a man, a handshake is all you need. If you don't trust him, all the paper in the world isn't going to help you."

# Take Political Action

Rathgeber holds that when a philanthropist attempts something of a political nature, he or she enters an entirely different world. He explains, "The rules are different, and new tactics are necessary. If politics are involved, the philanthropist has to look at the situation from every angle and figure out the point of view of every constituency, because somebody with a hidden agenda will be out there trying to mess up the game. Count on it. Also, it's always necessary to give politicians cover, because they don't want to offend any group of voters."

Rathgeber was first exposed to this rough-and-tumble world when he ran for a position on the Eanes Independent School District school board in the 1980s. "At that time, the Austin ISD was in the throes of a busing fiasco," he recalls. "To illustrate: our son, Ross, had always been a model student and then, the year he went to a sixth-grade learning center, he suddenly became a discipline problem. The AISD schools were crowded, and the learning center had been put together on the spur of the moment in an old abandoned school. Very little learning was taking place there. Ross had a teacher that year who was hard to respect. She could not send a note home without its having at least three spelling or grammatical errors.

"Furthermore, he was in class with Dale Mockford, his best friend since the three-year-old nursery school at U.T. The two boys were bright, and they quickly concluded that they knew more than their teacher did. That poor teacher was completely unable to cope with the boys." He chuckles. "When she came to class in the morning, she would just fill out detention slips with the boys' names on them, so all she had to do was write in the time of the offense. Fortunately the principal, Ruth Moses, was a friend of ours, and when the boys arrived in her office, she routinely sent them down to the library to tutor other kids.

"Well, Sara and I put up with this for two years and then, since I was developing Lost Creek at the time, we decided to move to the Lost Creek neighborhood so the kids could go into the Eanes ISD. We built a house on a beautiful lot overlooking the Barton Creek golf course. My dad, who had been a West Texas flatlander, saw our new place and he told my mother, 'I don't know what's gotten into that crazy kid. He doesn't have a single place to put a garden.'

"We'd been living there for about two years when one of the incumbents on the Eanes school board decided not to run for reelection. Several people suggested that I run for that spot, so I did. Getting elected was not too hard, and I enjoyed making a contribution to the schools. However, three years later, when it was time for me to run for reelection, a controversial bond election had recently passed by fewer than a hundred votes.

"Since I was the incumbent, I became the target of the

naysayers' ire. Initially I had two opponents, but after the first vote, one was eliminated, and that person endorsed me. There would be a runoff, but I was the underdog because I actually trailed the other candidate. School officials were very concerned. They felt I'd been an asset to the school board, and they said, 'Dick, we need you. You *have* to win.'

"It wasn't going to be easy, but I soon came up with an idea. I recruited approximately 150 people and asked them to make a list of at least ten people who had not voted in the first election. Next to their names were their phone numbers. Remember, this was before e-mail and the Internet, so we had to contact voters personally. We asked these 150 recruits to call their list of non-voters on the last day of early voting, as well as on the day of the election. Because of this effort, I wound up winning sixty percent of the vote—but the experience was so harrowing that I made a deal with the Lord: if I got out of that mess with my reputation intact, I promised I would *never* run for office again.

"That runoff election got nasty. People started spreading false rumors that I was getting kickbacks on the sale of school sites. There's no way to counter that. All you can say is, 'Hey, you know me better than that.' But the main thing is, I learned to stay out of the political arena."

Even with all the political infighting, though, Rathgeber felt he had made a positive contribution to the Eanes ISD. "As a school board member, I was very active in finding new school sites, as well as in helping sell school bonds to the public. At that time, prime interest rates were eighteen percent, and the market rate for school bonds was twelve percent. State law said that you could not sell bonds for over ten percent. The state wouldn't approve them for more than that. When the prime rate hits eighteen percent, it's easy enough to understand that no bank or financial institution would be interested in receiving less than ten percent for the purchase of a bond, which in effect is a long-term obligation. Therefore, we were at a standstill, and we desperately needed to build two new elementary schools. That area was just exploding with growth, and there weren't enough schools to accommodate all the children."

The answer came to Dick in one of his middle-of-the-night ruminations. "I suddenly realized that the Eanes School District had been doing business with the old Austin National Bank for years and years," he says, "and I knew, from my business experience, about compensating balances. This is the amount of money you keep in a non-interest-bearing account."

It didn't hurt that Rathgeber had some good friends at the bank. "The next morning I got Don Rogers, Eanes ISD superintendent, and Jesse Bohls, who was the school district's business manager, to go with me to visit Leon Stone at the Austin National Bank. Before we went, I contacted Mr. Stone and asked that he have his financial number crunchers with him at the meeting. I asked the bankers to compute the amount that we would need to leave as a compensating balance in order for them to bid on our bonds at under ten percent. We shook hands on an amount, and we provided that compensating balance from the general operating funds of the school district. When we opened bids, Austin National Bank was the only bidder, and their rate was under ten percent. Our gentleman's agreement provided that, once rates went back down, the compensating balance requirement would go away. Problem solved.

"Some months later, we again needed to sell some

bonds, but this time, Austin National was underbid by a rival bank without any compensating balances having been discussed. It's not that the economy had changed. It's just that the newer bank needed something in its investment portfolio, and its officers were willing to take a lower rate of return. The bottom line is that we were able to build new schools in a very adverse financial climate."

In the end, Rathgeber says, he learned two important lessons from his brief political career: "First, there's always more than one way to skin a cat. And second, I'm going to stay the heck out of politics."

STAYING THE HECK OUT OF POLITICS, of course, doesn't mean Rathgeber skirts the political arena if he's determined to get something done. Take Northeast Travis County Park, for example, in eastern Travis County. County commissioner Ron Davis tells the story:

"There was an outcry among my constituents for a park, and there was no doubt we needed a park in eastern Travis County. Briarcreek, a starter-home subdivision, was being developed and the area was booming with growth. In 2003-2004, we had held a bond election, which passed, and this allowed the money to buy the land for the park. But it didn't provide enough money to make the necessary improvements. We had applied for a grant from Texas Parks and Wildlife, but we were turned down for lack of private participation.

"Then the people started asking me for something that I couldn't deliver: a swimming pool. We barely had enough money for a park, and we certainly didn't have the funds for a pool. I kept saying that I might be able to get them a park, but *no* county park had a swimming pool. That was just the way things were. But people kept after me, so finally I had the idea of approaching Mr. Rathgeber, who I knew was a partner in developing Briarcreek, for advice.

"I explained to him that citizens in eastern Travis County had to drive twenty or thirty miles to swim. The closest pool was in Bastrop. I told him the story of how we were turned down for lack of private funding and how we kept hitting dead ends. He heard me out and then he said, 'I'll give you the private participation. I'll make a contribution of $125,000, and I'll see what else I can scare up.'

"Well, he went to the company that was building the houses in the subdivision, D.R. Horton, and persuaded them to contribute $375,000. After that, because we had met their requirement for private funds, we received a $500,000 grant from Texas Parks and Wildlife.

"Mr. Rathgeber said, 'Every kid should have the right to swim in these hot Texas summers.' He got the YMCA involved, so we have a unique, three-way operational system involving the Briarcreek Homeowners Association, whose members pay a nominal fee to become members; the Y, which actually manages the pool; and the county, on whose property the pool is situated. So it is a public/private cooperative effort. I would add that nonmembers can swim there as well.

"What we have today is an Olympic-size pool and another pool for children. I'm pleased to report that the county has not had to subsidize the pool, because it generates enough money to operate. It's used by plenty of people. My precinct is between Manor and the newly incorporated Webberville, a big, growing area that's full of new development. We couldn't have found a better site, or a greater need, for a swimming pool.

"This will be our third summer in operation, but I often remember when we had the ribbon-cutting ceremony. The children wanted us to hurry up and cut the ribbon because they wanted to go swimming. We almost had a stampede on our hands!"

Commissioner Davis says working with Rathgeber has changed the way he does business. "I'm no longer hesitant to ask the business community for help. This arrangement was a winner for everybody involved. It was a good deal for D.R. Horton, because they were able to offer homebuyers swimming privileges for $6.50 a month per family. The usual YMCA annual family membership fee is $150 a year, and even if a family could afford that, there wasn't a pool anywhere around.

"I've never met anyone like Mr. Rathgeber," he says. "I thought there was no way we could get a pool in a county park, but he wouldn't let precedent stop him. He just has a way of making things happen, things that nobody is expecting. He reminds me of a snapping turtle. They grab hold of something in the daytime hours and they won't turn loose until the sun goes down. That's the kind of person he is— a power broker, but one who operates behind the scenes. When all is said and done, though, it's his input that makes things happen."

THERE IS A TEACHER in the Austin Independent School District who would agree. Carol Nelson has taught band at McCallum High School for twenty-eight years. She is greatly respected by her students and their parents, and her band has won many awards. But this year, through meeting Dick Rathgeber, she learned how far her influence can extend.

She starts at the beginning: "For many, many years—since the 1970s—the music faculty and staff, as well as the parents of band kids in the AISD, have been trying to have a performing arts center built for our outstanding students to showcase their talents. We've never had a suitable place for students to perform, even though we have highly talented students in music, dance, and theater. Here at McCallum, for example, we have an auditorium that seats only 280 people. This means that all our big concerts and contests have to be held in outlying communities such as Leander, Westlake, Hays, or Round Rock. Ironically, those smaller communities have good venues for major performances. While AISD bands and orchestra do very well at contests, we have never had the home court advantage."

This need is widely recognized in the city. In fact, Austin citizens approved a bond for a new performing arts center in 2004, generating $8.8 million. However, use of the funds was contingent on finding matching funds.

Nelson says, "I was on a committee to explore sites. We considered becoming partners with the Long Center for our performances, but we immediately recognized that this presented problems. For one thing, there wasn't adequate parking. For another, the facility didn't quite meet our needs. Ultimately, the district decided not to enter a joint venture between the AISD and the Long Center. With that, we were back to square one, and the designated $8.8 million remained unused, sitting in an account somewhere."

In November 2007, Nelson went to Rochester, New York, to hear one of her former students, Amanda Muskin, give a performance at the Eastman School of Music. She was traveling with Amanda's mother, Ellen, and in the course of their conversations on that trip, Ellen asked what was really needed for the music program at McCallum. "A performing arts center," Nelson replied, feeling like a broken record. How many times had she and other music teachers asked? Begged? Pleaded?

But this time was different. She explains, "A couple of days after that trip, Alan Muskin, Ellen's husband, called and asked me if I could meet with him and a friend of his named Dick Rathgeber. He asked me to bring the McCallum Fine Arts Academy coordinator, Lanier Bayliss, and meet them at the Headliners Club downtown. I said sure, but I didn't have high expectations."

Over lunch, Rathgeber made a most unexpected proposal. "He said he wanted to give the school district a big piece of land at the Mueller development site for a district-wide performing arts center. Five acres! 'We need to make this happen,' he said. After lunch, we went to the Mueller office and saw the model. Talk about fired up! I just couldn't believe it. I came back to school and called my AISD supervisor, Dr. John May, and I also called Vince Torres, our school board representative from this area. We were all so excited and hopeful.

"As I understand it, Mr. Rathgeber had already contacted the school district before he talked to us, but nothing much had been done."

That initial meeting took place in mid-November, and it soon became clear that Rathgeber wasn't finished with Carol Nelson. She says, "In January, he called and said, 'We need to get moving on this. If you want a performing arts center, you need to create a tsunami of support.' I agreed with him, but I had no idea how to go about it. So he began to coach me. In a subsequent conversation, he said, 'There's a committee, a citizens' advisory committee, that's set up to figure out the district's needs and address them. Two of these meetings are coming up, and we need to get people mobilized to be there.' He said further that if we didn't get the issue on the bond election, it was dead.

"Of course, as a district employee, I cannot really tell people to vote or make people do anything, but what I *can* do is make people aware of issues affecting their children. So I began calling band directors and letting them in on what was happening. I told them the first thing we needed to do was get the issue in the upcoming bond election. Through my band director friends, we were able to get band parents involved. The McCallum band parents played a really integral role. They gave speeches, informed people via e-mail, made personal contact, and made sure we had people speaking to the citizens' bond advisory committee, or CBAC. Other fine arts parents from around the school district spoke as well."

Nelson spoke, too, but she couldn't give an opinion. "I just stated the facts," she says, "but the facts are persuasive. This issue of a performing arts center was becoming a passion of mine, and a passion of our band parents. Even so, in the end, the CBAC didn't put our issue in the bond package because a group of planners for the Mueller development site felt we were rushing it through. They held that we hadn't gone through the proper process.

"That's the point at which many people would have given up, but Rathgeber said, 'No, let's keep pushing.' The CBAC had to go to the school board to make their recommendations, and in their report they said that there had been considerable support for a performing arts center but that they hadn't put it in the bond package. Once again the AISD school board held some planning meetings, and again the public was invited to attend and provide input. You can guess what happened. We descended on them in force—and we were all carrying signs."

Teachers, school musicians, and parents continued to speak up about the need for a performance venue. Mollie Tower, a retired music teacher and former AISD administrator, helped recruit influential people to speak at the school board meetings in support of the issue. For example, at one of the meetings, Paula Crider stood up to speak. Crider is a well-known former U.T. band director who conducts around the world, and she made an impassioned pitch to the board. "We've been asking for this for decades!" she said. "Please help us."

Nelson says, "Meanwhile, Mr. Rathgeber was calling me and letting me know what was going on behind the scenes. He coached me on what points we needed to make at these hearings, and our turnout was just massive. Just to make our presence known, I attended every meeting and I always stayed until the very end.

"If we were late in getting the issue of a performing arts center into the bond package for the next election, nobody told Mr. Rathgeber that. About half of the people who spoke at those meetings spoke about how much we needed a performance venue. Somehow, knowing that Mr. Rathgeber was on our side, we gradually came to believe we were going to be successful. Mr. Rathgeber holds a person accountable, but you like it because you feel effective.

"The result was that the school board put the performing arts center in the bond package. All along, my band parents and others throughout the entire school district had been saying, 'If you can get it on the ballot, we'll pass it.'

And they did! Cathy Purdy, parent of an Anderson Band member, was very instrumental in getting the vote out. She amassed e-mail lists from band parents, orchestra parents, PTAs, neighborhood associations, and countless other groups. These e-mail lists were activated to make sure that supporters of the performing arts center and the rest of the school bonds voted. And vote they did. The bonds passed with flying colors! Proposition Three included the performing arts center, and it passed by sixty-nine percent. This would never have happened if Mr. Rathgeber had not been so determined."

Rathgeber is donating the land and giving another $2.5 million to the cause, and it has been determined that this will suffice as matching funds for the $8.8 million already held in trust for a center. Asked about this uphill battle, Rathgeber says, "To me it seemed like a piece of cake. The need was so obvious. If they had the land and a little additional help, what could stop them?"

But to Carol Nelson it still seems miraculous. "What's interesting is that I've never really been involved in making a difference like this," she says, "but Mr. Rathgeber empowered me. He could have called anybody, but he called me. He believed in me. If someone believes in you, you just live up to their expectations."

## Alice Blue Gown

Carol Nelson says, "In a frivolous moment, I had promised Mr. R. that if the bond issue passed, we would play a song just for him at our annual spring band concert. He said he wanted to hear a waltz called *Alice Blue Gown,* because that was the song that they played when he was in the army just before the end of the parade. After that song was played, you got to go home. He said the tradition in the army is that the band plays the commander's favorite song right before you march in review. In Mr. Rathgeber's case, the song was *Alice Blue Gown*. I didn't know the song, and we had a devil of a time finding the music. Finally we located it through the archives of the Marine Band in Washington, D.C. They faxed us the music and we began practicing it immediately. Some of my more enterprising students set up a bubble machine in the rear of the band to look like the set of the Lawrence Welk show.

When the evening of the concert arrived, I introduced Mr. Rathgeber, and he asked the crowd to give me a standing ovation for the part I had played in making the performing arts center a reality. This was the first time I had ever gotten a standing ovation in my entire career, and I think Mr. Rathgeber was every bit as pleased as I was that night.

I will remember that for the rest of my life.

*Sara and Dick Rathgeber, 2006*

*The Rathgeber family on an African photo safari, 1985*

*Rathgeber family portrait, 1987*

—Photo by Gray Hawn

*Dick and Sara with Lady Bird Johnson at a fundraiser for the Lady Bird Johnson Wildflower Center*

# Random Thoughts from Rathgeber

If you have gotten this far in reading this book, you've probably figured out that I have strong opinions about family, work, charity, faith, ethics, personal integrity, politics, and friendship, to name just a few general subjects.

Even though I didn't write this book to share my opinions, the reader can be forgiven for wanting to know a little more about how I think. The stories here might illustrate how I *act* in certain situations, but in this last section I'd like to share something about my core beliefs. My reasoning is simple: I want to pass on what I have learned during my life, and I hope someone, somewhere, will pick up the ball that I've tried to carry regarding charitable giving.

I can't overestimate the joy that comes from helping people and organizations that really need help. If you've been fortunate enough to be born in this country, and if you have had the vast good luck to accumulate some material gain during your work life, I believe you need to share that. If you don't have all that much money, I still think you need to share. Whatever your circumstances, there are people

174

who need your assistance, and even more importantly, you need to give for your own benefit. You will grow from giving. Your life will gain significance, and you'll be a happier, more fulfilled person. This I believe.

## On Raising Children

If you want smart kids, you need to start out by getting them a smart mama. Scientists say the brains come from the mother, and that's why I believe the axiom that a family will go from riches to rags in three generations. It's a true fact, and here's why: in the first generation, the father will work his head off to make a fortune. Of course, it could be the mother who works for the material gain, but for the sake of my illustration, let's stick with the father.

So he works hard to make his fortune. In the second generation, the son will often be a playboy who marries the blonde, beautiful, buxom, and brainless cheerleader.

After that, the third generation doesn't have a chance, because they didn't get the brains. There you have it: riches to rags in three generations.

But say you have the good luck to avoid that scenario. Here's another little bit of wisdom I would pass along. It's about leaving inheritances. In my view, you should teach your children to fish, but do not give them fish—because fish spoil. Give your children all the education that they will absorb, but don't hand over money. That's a mistake.

Once Sara and I were in New Zealand, and I struck up a conversation with a psychologist who helped me understand why this is true. I told her that I could not understand why some friends of ours were estranged from their daughter. "She won't even speak to her parents," I said, "and they have given her everything that she could possibly need or want."

The psychologist replied, "Oh, Mr. Rathgeber, that's easy. It's called dependency resentment."

My advice to parents is never to stifle the ambitions of children or grandchildren. Let them make their own way. Believe they can do it. They'll love you for it.

What this means is that a parent has to be willing to let his or her children fail. It won't hurt them in the long run. After all, you can't raise an oak tree in a greenhouse. What makes an oak tree strong is that it puts down deep roots, and what makes it put down roots is that it gets blown by the wind. However, if it gets too much wind, it will be up-rooted. The trick as a parent is to calculate how much wind, metaphorically speaking, is enough. You can protect the young tree from gales of wind, but never try to keep it from exposure to wind.

## About Marriage

I've been thinking recently about why some marriages work, while so many others fail. I'm a big fan of Dr. Joyce Brothers, the noted psychologist. Dr. Brothers says that for a marriage to work, the woman has to respect the man, and the man has to absolutely adore the woman. Otherwise he's going to keep looking.

And here's an interesting statistic for you. Church leaders say that while half of marriages end in divorce, if the couple will attend church together three Sundays out of four, those odds go up to one in 431.

Another thing: Spouses should never, never, ever criticize each other in public.

## Giving Speeches

They say a picture is worth a thousand words. If you're giving a speech and you can paint a word picture in ten words, you've just saved 990 words and increased the chances that somebody in your audience is actually going to listen to what you have to say.

Another piece of advice is to be extremely careful with the use of humor. The key is to know your audience. For example, I once told a story that was only slightly off-color at a statewide Salvation Army meeting, and it absolutely bombed. Since then, when in doubt, I keep it clean.

## Doing Business

A friend of mine, Nash Phillips, is a big Austin builder. He likes to say that all his life he has heard this person or that one described as arrogant, snooty, or stuck up. However, he says he never has met anybody like that—but he has met some insecure SOBs. That's a good thing to keep in mind when doing business with a difficult person.

I've said it before, and I'll say it again: Return all calls within fifteen minutes, and return the dreaded ones first. In my opinion, the most common trait among successful people may be that they return phone calls promptly.

Motivate people. Encourage others to realize their untapped potential. This is one of life's greatest joys, and it's accomplished when you learn to delegate authority. Never do anything that someone else can do as well—and maybe even better.

Accept the fact that the most terrible truth is never as bad as uncertainty. Know when to "let 'er burn." Here's what I mean. When my dad was eight or nine years old, he went to school in Wichita Falls, and he had to walk back and forth to school every day. One winter day, when it was about twenty degrees and the wind was blowing about thirty miles an hour, an older boy of eleven or twelve found an old cigar butt. He went behind a straw pile to light it. He dropped the match, and soon the straw pile started burning. The boy whipped off his coat and tried to beat out the fire, but it took hold quickly. The more the boy fought the fire, the higher the flames shot.

Finally, with flames shooting fifty to sixty feet in the air, the young man stepped back and said, "I'm going to let 'er burn."

A lot of situations in life are like that. We have absolutely no control over them.

When it comes to buying, selling, or renting, I have to say that the best salesman I ever observed was a retired small town school superintendent. I called him Uncle Henry, and I learned a tremendous amount about buying and selling from him. When buying, he said, you should never make the first offer.

It was also fun to watch him rent a house. Uncle Henry would never show a rent house until he could get two or three people there at the same time. He would manage to arrive about five minutes late, then he would rush in, look at the potential renters, and say, "Okay, who's first?" This gave the impression of competition.

Here's another thing: never, ever negotiate by e-mail. We were recently in the middle of negotiations for a sizable contract when we received an e-mail from the client asking us to cut our price by $400,000. Instead of replying by e-mail, we asked for a face-to-face meeting. When we sat down, we learned that our competitor had underbid us by a large amount. However, several items were included in our bid that our competitor had deliberately left out. The client agreed that these services were necessary and should be included, and when these services were figured in, we were within $60,000 of their bid. That was easy to resolve, and needless to say, we got the job.

This one is simple: never lie. Just tell the truth. You can tell the truth ninety-nine times and lie once, but the only thing people will ever remember is the time you told a lie. Also, if you tell the truth, you never have to remember what you said.

Never co-sign a note. If you absolutely, positively have to help somebody buy something, guarantee the note and ask the bank to agree to turn the collateral over to you if the deal goes in the ditch.

Be absolutely dependable. Say what you are willing to do, and then do what you said you would.

Use what I call the "third-man theme." If someone asks you to lower your price, or do something you don't want to do, just say, "I don't think my partner would agree to that."

Always treat people fairly. You can shear a sheep a bunch of times, but you can only skin him once.

## Charitable Giving:

Remember to let the press help you mold public opinion. This is what they do, and their help is invaluable.

Expect some criticism. Oftentimes the criticism is what I call "pocketbook protection." And anyway, as my mama used to say, "The moon doesn't change its course for the barking of the dogs."

When doing charitable work in a foreign country, try to form partnerships wherein you buy the material and the local people do the work. Give a hand up, not a hand out.

In bringing other people into your charitable projects, there's a fine line between being persistent and being a pest. I'm afraid that at times I have crossed the line. But my motto is "Keep on knockin'." I say the first two no's don't count, because most people say no seven times before they say yes. You have to find a way to ask the same question repeatedly without being annoying. (And if you're annoying, don't worry about it.)

If you're supporting a charity, you need to recognize that there will be times when you need to support causes that you know very little about, and with which you wouldn't necessarily be enamored. But keep in mind that if you're asking for the help of a key person, you need to pay your dues. In other words, if I'm asking someone to support my cause, that person has the right to ask me to support his. Never, ever permit anyone to make a solicitation unless they have, themselves, committed. The solicitor won't get anything, and he or she might waste a good prospect.

According to my good friend, Gary Farmer, an asker needs to earn the right to ask.

Always ask for a significant amount. I once targeted a prospect for $250,000. At our campaign meeting, the president of the bank said, "I'll take him." Who was I to argue? At the next meeting, the banker proudly announced, "I got his check for $5,000." That is what I call leaving money on the table.

## The Good Life

Call at least two old people every day. It will make them feel good, and it will make you feel even better.

Give everybody a smile. Help others to be the best they can be.

Don't drink alcohol at parties, but always have a soft drink with a twist of lime in your hand. People are uncomfortable if they're drinking and they think you're not. If you stay sober, you'll avoid embarrassing yourself, and sometimes you get really good information.

Don't forget, it's no sin to be knocked down. The sin comes from failing to get back up.

You don't learn to sail on a calm sea. People learn from adversity.

However, storms never last. Get through to the better day tomorrow.

The End